# LIVE
## YOUR ASSIGNMENT

Being Christ's Ambassador
in 7 Spheres of Life

PHIL M. WAGLER

Live Your Assignment
Copyright ©2023 Phil Wagler

Published by Castle Quay Books
Burlington, Ontario, Canada and Jupiter, Florida, U.S.A.
416-573-3249 | info@castlequaybooks.com | www.castlequaybooks.com

Printed in Canada and the USA.

Image of a puddle by Shelley Simpson (2022). Used with permission.

Edited by Marina Hofman, PhD
Cover design and book interior by Burst Impressions

978-1-988928-94-4 Soft Cover
978-1-988928-95-1 E-book

**Library and Archives Canada Cataloguing in Publication**
Title: Live your assignment: being Christ's ambassador in 7 spheres of life / by Phil M Wagler.
Names: Wagler, Phil M., author.
Description: Includes bibliographical references.
Identifiers: Canadiana 20230519423 | ISBN 9781988928944 (softcover)
Subjects: LCSH: Christian life. | LCSH: Theology, Practical.
Classification: LCC BV4501.3 .W34 2023 | DDC 248.4—dc23

CASTLE QUAY BOOKS

*For Raymond and Margaret.*

*My Dad and Mom, who modeled simple faithfulness*
*in their assignments to the end.*

# THANKSGIVING

There aren't enough words to thank my wife, Jen, for her patience and love. She lives her assignments so well and is always a model to me of Christlike faithfulness. She is my best friend. After thirty years of marriage, I appreciate her more and more, and we continue to be reminded daily of the importance of our household assignment through our children, who always keep us honest and humble. So, I thank each of them too—Caleb, Benjamin, Jessie, Sadie, Micah, and Abigail. All amazing. All with their own assignments. All a gift to their mom, me, and the world.

Thank you as well to:

- My friends at Multiply, whose disciple-making influence and global heart birthed these ideas.

- The believers of all ages and assignments in the churches I have been privileged to serve and grow with who taught me about faithful witness in Wellesley, Ayr, Edson, Zurich, Clinton, Surrey, Langley, and Kelowna.

- The leadership of Kelowna Gospel Fellowship Church for encouraging me to write this for others.

- The World Evangelical Alliance's Peace & Reconciliation Network global team for growing me as a minster of reconciliation.

- My colleagues at the Evangelical Fellowship of Canada for their yearning to see the church be a blessing to the country God assigned me to.

- The partners whose generosity and spurring helped make this work possible.

PHIL WAGLER

• The Castle Quay Books team for their kindness and expertise.

• You the reader for caring about how your life assignments matter to God and considering these ideas worthy of giving your time and energy.

And, most of all,

"Give thanks to the Lord, for he is good;
his love endures forever."

Psalm 118:1

# CONTENTS

# PROLOGUE
## (OR, AN UNEXPECTED PARADE IN THE PARK)

An annual multicultural festival took place in our Canadian city every summer. Various ethnicities proudly displayed their heritage, arts, language, and glorious, savory food. A woman from our church was on the planning committee, and she was determined to have me in my role as a pastor involved too. I didn't know what she had in mind.

It was a hot July day, and I had been working outside wearing a grubby pair of shorts, T-shirt and baseball cap. Not wanting to miss the festival, I didn't bother changing as we quickly packed up the clan and headed to the park. Once there, we bumped into our fellow church member—a bubbly Malagasy sister in Christ. She was excited to see us and immediately said, "Follow me. Now!"

We had intended this as a family summer excursion. But my wife and I looked at each other, discerned the moment, and shrugged, and off I went, leaving my wife with four kids while I took a daughter with me. Our friend guided us to a fenced-off area that required special VIP clearance, which she had, and we stepped into another world: a city festival holy of holies. I was now surrounded by suits, ties, and fancy dresses. In my ripped shorts, dirt-marked T-shirt, and tattered baseball cap, I was happily introduced to the mayor of the city, provincial and parliamentary politicians, the consuls general of China and Ukraine, and a host of other dignitaries assembled for the festival's official opening ceremonies. I was feeling very out of place as they courteously greeted this commoner and his peasant daughter. I was sure that was the end, but we were just getting started.

Someone official with a walkie-talkie bellowed for attention: "All right, everyone, follow me!" Soon we were caught in a tidal wave of the dignified, ascending stairs that opened onto the platform of the main pavilion. The official opening ceremonies were about to begin, and there I was—grubby clothes and a ten-year-old in hand—standing with legislators, a mayor, and diplomats, trying to not look out of place as we stood before a vast throng who no doubt wondered how that guy and that girl crashed the party!

It felt as if we stood there forever. A sense of awkwardness overwhelmed me. I just wanted to reunite with my family, who were out there somewhere in the crowd, dumbfounded. The obligatory speeches finally concluded with a smattering of polite applause. Surely now we would be free! But no, this had all just been the appetizer.

Now came the official parade of nations, which of course the assembled dignitaries—my daughter and I included—were to lead! We descended among the crowds, the masses parting like the Red Sea as we marched up and down the long rows of national displays. We passed our Malagasy friend—waving and giving the thumbs up! We sauntered past my wife, surrounded by hot, cranky kids, staring at me and wondering what in the name of falafel and empanadas was going on. I shrugged and just kept walking—there was no graceful exit at this point.

The parade wound its way through the park and ended at the official reception tent for VIPs. The rest of the family caught up, and together we flowed into this cool, covered space where milk, honey, and wine flowed. The kids were thrilled with all the goodies (not the wine)! As we settled in and began conversations, it suddenly dawned on me that this, all along, had been our friend's intention: to get us to this place where we could strike up conversations with people who had titles but were simple human beings with not-so-simple problems.

One man began talking about the challenges of parenting.

A woman starting spilling about the death of her marriage.

A diplomat talked about the challenges his people were facing in the city.

There were amazing conversations and the opportunity for us in our common, summer-holiday shorts and shirts to be Christians—to listen, care, pay attention, quietly pray, and speak hope. We were able as a household, kids included, to be the presence of Jesus. An assignment became clear in that moment. I had not planned or strategized it. I simply needed to wake up, literally be pushed to walk into it, and accept the limits of the moment and the unexpected area of influence our heavenly Father had made possible (with a little help from his Malagasy daughter).

# CHAPTER 1
# REST IN GOD'S SOVEREIGNTY

God has assignments for each of us, and for us together.

What areas of influence has God given to you?

What life assignments are unique to you, in this moment in history, with the limits that are part of being a human being in a big, complex world?

You didn't choose when or where you would be born. You didn't choose your birth story, adoption story, or skin colour or the society you arrived in. Perhaps you have risen from poverty to riches. Perhaps you have gone from affluence to need. Perhaps an accident or disability meant talk of becoming anything you want to has become a cruel joke. Perhaps you find yourself in a season of life that is frustrating and unfulfilling or seems like one grand misadventure of missteps, mistakes, and misalignments. Most of life is not like the movies. Most of life is drudgery, the same old same old smattered with moments of clarity and breakthrough on the one hand and unwelcome interruptions and detours on the other.

Does God have an assignment for us regardless of where we find ourselves? Or are we just paddling with regret and impatience while we wait for some rapturous breakthrough moment that may never come? Are we left comparing our reality to the "perfect" life social media depicts other people having? Do we simply give in to our impatience and make our own way?

I recall a young man at the college my wife and I worked at. He was completely unsettled with student life when the world was a mess and needed saving. He was gifted, charismatic, and visionary. He saw what could and should be done after a few semesters and concluded that he knew what he needed to know and was done with waiting. So he quit and launched out boldly and brashly. A few years later, however, he had flamed out and had burned bridges and lost his influence.

We are repeatedly tempted to believe that more and faster is better. The pasture is always greener somewhere else. We should reach for the stars, embrace positive thinking, become all we can, break down every barrier that stands in our way, and chase our dreams.

On the one hand there is truth to this. We should steward our lives fully to the greatest capacity God has given. We should not waste our limited breath. You only live once. You have one shot, one span of years, so don't squander it. There is holy wisdom there.

But a subtle and powerful lie creeps in and deceives us when we choose the road of self-determination. We believe the best is somewhere else, that real winners push hard and make things happen even at the expense of others. When this lie becomes our truth, what is hard and right-in-front-of-us becomes a barrier or a block to "real" self-determination and success (like completing an education being a barrier, or your family being a stumbling block to your success and freedom, or today's challenges being bothersome obstacles to the life that the movies, commercials, or progress seduces you to live).

We all know someone—or might be that someone—who constantly glances past the people they are with. Have you ever tried to talk with someone like that? You're talking, but they are looking somewhere else. You're at dinner, and they are texting with someone else. They look past you. You are there, but not to them. We can treat our lives this way when there are assignments, responsibilities, and spheres of influence right in front of us, yet we're looking somewhere else. We can miss the life we have while chasing an illusion or caricature. We end up grasping the wind.

What if the assignments God has given us are simpler, clearer, and more transformative than we've imagined? What if God, in his wisdom, has assignments for us that—if understood and embraced—will result in more joy, fulfillment, contentment, and influence than we've imagined? What if we're simply meant—sometimes in our tattered summer clothes—to step into moments, places, and geographies we inhabit and be Christian right there: redeemed in Christ, clothed in Christ, at peace in Christ, and sent by Christ?

Step out of your comfort zone and read out loud these words of Jesus: "You did not choose me, but I chose you and appointed you so that you might go and bear fruit—fruit that will last" (John 15:16).

Jesus chooses disciples and appoints them to bear lasting fruit in the world. Christian theology declares the hopeful mystery that God is sovereign over all that is: the past, present, and future. As Christians we accept, at least in theory, that God is sovereign over our lives. Jesus is *the* Lord and *my* Lord. My "choosing" to follow Jesus is always precipitated by the wonder that he chose me. The wonderful mystery that God has chosen us by grace comes with the joyful expectation and responsibility to produce what the Spirit of God has planted in our lives: the character of God and the works of God. God chooses and assigns us for a purpose: to be fruit producers. Christians are appointed to tend our lives toward what pleases God and reveals his holy character and sovereign rule wherever we are. Our assignment is not somewhere else or someone else. God chose our assignments and their fruitful purpose right here, right now.

Jesus also said, "'Peace be with you! As the Father has sent me, I am sending you.' And with that he breathed on them and said, 'Receive the Holy Spirit'" (John 20:21–22).

Jesus speaks peace over the lives of his disciples. He does not demand striving, guilted obligation, or anxiety-producing self-determination. The launch pad for our assignments as ambassadors of the kingdom of God is shalom: the peace of God himself. We live our assignments from restful awareness of being children of God. We do not have to prove ourselves. Furthermore, Jesus gives the Holy Spirit, sending us into our assignments with the same presence and power he was sent with.

Ambassadors carry a great and noble responsibility. Diplomats are sent to represent what their leader is proposing, how they see the world, and what their purposes are for advancing their concerns. An ambassador stands in as if they were the country they represent—even at summer festivals. They come with the limits their leader has set for them. They come in peace, carrying diplomatic privilege, authority to represent their Sender, and freedom to be who they are. They can't, however, make up their own agenda. When they arrive in their assignment, it is just as if the president, prime minister, or sovereign of that other country has arrived.

We are sent-ones. We are ambassadors of the King of kings.

The key to living our sent-ness—our ambassadorial assignment—is understanding how Jesus was sent. Jesus arrived by God's sovereign timing into a particular place, at a particular time, and among a particular people. Perhaps we don't think of it this way, but Jesus's life as the Son of God was limited by the Father's will, and Jesus accepted that.

He wasn't sent to Rome.

He wasn't born in the emperor's palace.

His celebrity could not spread through social media.

Galatians 4:4 says, "When the right time came, God sent his Son, born of a woman, subject to the law." For our salvation Jesus was sent, and he was sent with limits. Even a human body was a limiting factor for God, who is Spirit. It was his obedience to the Father's will within those limits that unleashed salvation (Philippians 2:6–11 NLT). The cross itself set a clear limit for Jesus. He wrestled with the Father over this: "Take this from me! Make another way! Nevertheless, not my will, but yours be done" (see Matthew 26:39). Jesus—God in human flesh—was sent with limits set for him, and he submitted. It brought him pleasure to do the Father's will. And it was his acceptance of the limits that made resurrection possible.

We are sent as he was sent, into limits and realities where we are to be ambassadors of heaven. But to do so means, as it did for Jesus, surrender. We must die to self. "If any of you wants to be my follower, you must give up your own way, take up your cross, and follow me. If you try to hang on to your life, you will lose it. But if you give up your life for my sake, you will save it. And what do you benefit if you gain the whole world but lose your own soul? Is anything worth more than your soul" (Matthew 16:24–26 NLT).

Do you notice the ambassadorial weight of this? If you try to hang on to life and try to gain the whole world (i.e., the self-made, self-determining life), you will lose. The only way to truly live, said Jesus, who modeled it, is to accept the limits of the cross-life: the life surrendered to and bordered by God's sovereign choice and purpose. To die to self is to rest in peace and discover true life. This is, counter-intuitively, the paramount way of valuing your soul; the fullness of who you are. Also, to live as sent-ones means breathing in the presence and power of the Holy Spirit. The same Spirit that raised Jesus from the dead is the only way in which we can be fully alive in the places God has for us. As Os Guinness writes in *The Call*, "The truth is not that God is finding us a place for our gifts but that God has created us and our gifts for the place of his choosing—and we will only be ourselves when we are finally there."[1]

So what if—as we receive God's marvelous assignments—we rest, yoked to Jesus, and find ourselves part of God's incredible plan to fill the universe with his glory?

Are you aware of the assignments God has given you?

What does it mean to be Christian in those assignments?

How will you embrace the assignments God has chosen to place you in right now?

Answering these questions is what this book is aimed at. Our hope is to awaken, receive with joy, and steward with care the assignments God has already given us. Our assignment is to be fully Christian

---

[1] Os Guinness, *The Call: Finding and Fulfilling the Central Purpose of Your Life* (Nashville: Thomas Nelson, 1998), 10.

where God sends and bear fruit that will last so that God's glory fills the universe.

The Bible reveals three truths about Sovereign God that we can rely on and find peace in:

### Sovereign God Has Set Limits on Our Lives.

> "You have decided the length of our lives. You know how many months we will live, and we are not given a minute longer." (Job 14:5 NLT)

Life is short. Isn't this what the elderly tell the rest of us? There is birth. There is toddler-ing. There is the exuberance of youth. There is puberty. There is the maturity that comes with growing up, making mistakes, and settling down. There is trouble. There is joy. There is a lot we can and probably should do with our short lives, but we didn't create them, and we can't predict what will take place even if we have the best education, lots of money, vibrant health, or a certified life coach. Our lives are limited. We live with boundaries we didn't create, and many of these we won't pass. We are born into a particular time with its unique opportunities, troubles, and challenges. Based on the law of averages, within seventy to eighty years our breath will expire, and we will die—sometimes because of the troubles and challenges of the historical moment we did not choose. We are blessed—or some may feel cursed—with a unique genealogy and ethnicity. We may move—or be moved—by circumstances outside our control. We will always be products of our time, family of origin, and the history of the people we didn't choose.

Job, just like us, protests and asks God to give him a break from this reality. "Look away … and leave us alone," he dismays (Job 14:6 NCV). That's human. Yet, Job's honest lament acknowledges our shared human story. It was, after all, our human rebellion against God's best that led to the limiting of our days in Genesis 6:3. God has set limits because of our fallenness and uncanny capacity to use our days to make things worse. Still, Job's lament also acknowledges a hope to cling to even in suffering: God has set the moment and limits and for some reason seen fit to place me within them.

That's hard, but also settling—even purposeful. After all, if God has set boundaries, then he will also be present and active within those limits because we are his offspring and made in his image. Grounding this hope is the repeated chorus throughout Scripture: "Give thanks to the LORD for he is good. His love endures forever" (Psalm 136:1). It is not only that the Lord is sovereign, but that he is sovereignly good. God's character, purposes, and motives are always good and good forever—even within the limitations and tribulations of life. Life is short and limited. You can fight it or rest your weary soul here.

### Sovereign God Knows Us.

"O LORD, you have examined my heart and know everything about me.

You know when I sit down or stand up. You know my thoughts even when I'm far away." (Psalm 139:1–2 NLT)

The creator of heaven and earth knows us. God knows us and our short life and limits. He has hemmed us in and cornered us, says Psalm 139:5, so that he can lay his hand upon us. This should awaken holy fear and responsibility. The King of kings has his eye on us and knows our circumstance and frailty. This should beckon us from the soul-losing God-less life to the expectant God-ward life that is a wonder.

That's what David sings: "Such knowledge is too wonderful for me!" (Psalm 139:6). The whole of Psalm 139 marvels at the joyful, humbling wonder that our limited life is known by God. This awakens the startling invitation for God to search and know us and to lead us in his everlasting ways (139:23–24). We can rest our weary selves on the knowledge that we are known by Sovereign God.

### *Sovereign God's Boundaries Are Meant to Draw People to Seek Him.*

From one man [God] created all the nations throughout the whole earth. He decided beforehand when they should rise and fall, and he determined their boundaries. His purpose was for the nations to seek after God and perhaps feel their way toward him and find him—though he is not far from any of us. (Acts 17:26–27 NLT)

In Acts 17 the apostle Paul addresses the philosophers of Areopagus in Athens. These were smart people who loved ideas and theories about life and sought after truth. In this pluralistic setting Paul unwraps the biblical worldview of God's sovereign nature, which he sums up this way:

• *God created human beings with a common heritage and planned that people should inhabit his earth.* This is summary retelling of humanity's Genesis 1:26–28 origin, identity, and mandate.

• *God has allotted periods of times and boundaries for peoples and nations* ("nations" is the Greek word *ethnos*—the root of the English word "ethnicity"—referring not to countries or political states, but people groups with a common culture). God even planned their rising and falling. History shifts, governments change, and peoples migrate. What may seem arbitrary is not so random after all but is bordered by God's purpose and timing. Paul's point in the brief moment he has been granted is that God has allotted periods and places where peoples have influence. The question becomes, what will we do with it?

• *Sovereign God's ultimate purpose is that all peoples will seek him.* God longs for all to feel their way toward him through the haze of history and the mess created by human sin and rebellion. The nations are like someone groping in the dark for a light switch. Our heavenly Father yearns for us all to come back home. After all, he is not far from any of us. Sovereign God is near, in all allotted periods and places. That means right here and now we can rest. Despite all that is foggy frustrating, and bursting into flames, God is actively drawing people toward him.

### Finally, and Decisively, We Can Rest Here: In Jesus Christ, Sovereign God Is Holding It All Together.

"For through him God created everything in the heavenly realms and on earth.

He made the things we can see and the things we can't see—such as thrones, kingdoms, rulers, and authorities in the unseen world. Everything was created through him and for him.

He existed before anything else, and he holds all creation together." (Colossians 1:16–17)

The creator centered everything in Christ from the very beginning. Jesus was there creating. There is no power apart from his power. When he came in the limits of human flesh and a historical moment that aimed at the cross, Jesus was fully revealing what the unlimited God was like. All things were created through Jesus and for Jesus. He is the sovereign ruler of his people—the church—and he sets the agenda for his ambassadors. He is the first to be resurrected as a sign of Sovereign God's desire for all to overcome the scourge of death and rise as the new humanity. And this was all to fulfill Sovereign God's purpose to reconcile to himself all things in heaven and on earth; everything, everywhere, forevermore made right and restored, held together, put back together, and brought to shalom, peace, and friendship through Jesus Christ, God with us.

God over all. God for all. God with us.

Holy, holy, holy is the Lord God Almighty, who was and is and is to come.

Christ has died. Christ has risen. Christ will come again.

Christians believe something incredible: neither your world nor the cosmos is ever spinning out of control. It is in fact being held *from* spinning out of control by the grace of God revealed in Jesus Christ. It is this hope that sustains us, even today. This is our hope in the drudgery and conundrums of everyday. And this is our hope for the end of days when Christ comes to judge the living and the dead.

Resting in God's sovereignty is not wishful thinking. We have a sure hope because God is holding all things together in Jesus Christ, through whom death and evil stand judged and defeated. Resting in God's sovereignty is not fatalism. We don't just shrug off our assignments or act indifferently to what is before us, because in Christ we see what it looks like to truly live. We are sent as Jesus was sent. Peace, not anxiety, uncertainty, or fear is ours. Purpose, not aimless wandering through life, is ours. We rest in the sovereignty of God, who is good and whose love endures forever.

God has set limits on our lives.

God knows us.

God is drawing people to seek him.

In Jesus, God is holding it all together.

We begin to live our assignments by resting here.

Do I believe this? Am I Christian? If not, who am I? What do I believe is holding all this together? Is it all purposeless? Am I simply chasing meaninglessness for selfish aims, to prove myself, or to escape when the going gets tough? Or has the God of the universe, the great and holy One, the Ancient of Days, chosen and given us great assignments in simple places?

Regardless of our age, ethnicity, or gender, he is recruiting us so that his glory might fill the universe. What if the good news is that we don't have to plan the parade or push our way into it? What if, in accepting the limits, dying to ourselves, and offering ourselves to the glory of God, we discover we are already in the parade, sent there with the high responsibility as an ambassador of the King of kings?

# CHAPTER 2
## WHAT IS OUR ASSIGNMENT?

The small town I grew up in had an annual fall fair. Every September my elementary school cancelled classes so we could go for the full day. Besides the joy of believing we were fleecing school administration, we kids had two main assignments: First, we had been given a list of creations like artwork, woodworking, baking, stories, and even handwriting we could enter to be judged, ribboned, and awarded cash prizes! I loved the competition and expectation of that day. Second, we were all to participate in a parade through town that wound from the school parking lot to the fairgrounds. Every kid was invited to decorate their tricycle or bicycle and ride the main street amidst the floats and bands. I hated this. I just wanted to get to the fair and find out what I had won. Central to this small-town extravaganza was the belief that every kid had something to offer. You learned a lot about what made us all tick and the unknown talents that lived among us that the town could be proud of.

Everywhere we go—even in our summer grubbies—there we are. In every place and relationship, we show up with the fullness of who we are, and the real us will be revealed. So who are we in the parade that has swept us along? In every sphere of life, Christians are on a God-given assignment to spread the knowledge of Jesus everywhere. But what does this look like?

Living our assignments as Christians in the world begins by resting in the sovereignty of God, who is good and whose love endures forever. There is much in life we will not know or understand, much that will even fluster us. Yet the Christian hope is that the world is never spinning out of control. In Christ, the world is in truly good hands, and through the cross of Christ all things in heaven and on earth are being reconciled to God (Colossians 1:20). So we rest in this hope. And since we are the body of Christ, God's handiwork and household, we expect that somehow God wants all his kids to be part of his sovereign purposes and will.

When we begin from this place of rest, we can bring our best to the assignments God has given us. We can be free from striving or the culturally induced pressure of needing to make it up as we go along. We don't need to chase vague dreams of self-determination. We can joyfully be in the parade assigned for us, in this place, at this stage of life, embracing this moment and its limits. This doesn't mean—as we will discover—that we don't seek new opportunities for the glory of God. It simply means we pay attention to first things and first places—to the parade marked out for us in the place God has seen fit to put us.

Jesus said to the first disciples, "You did not choose me, but I chose you and appointed you so that you might go and bear fruit—fruit that will last" (John 15:16). Jesus chose disciples before they chose him to bear the fruit of God's kingdom in the world he is reconciling. It is he who calls and sends us. There is a parade we are already in. We don't have to look for one.

Who are we in the parade? That is the question. To answer this vital question, let us consider what Paul said to the Christians in the Greek city of Corinth around the middle of the first century, "We, however, will not boast beyond proper limits, but will confine our boasting to the sphere of service God himself has assigned to us, a sphere that also includes you" (2 Corinthians 10:13).

Paul was boasting (the Greek word is *kauxaomai,* which means living with one's head held high). Is it OK to boast?

I recall landing my first paper route as a pre-teen. I was assigned a task, and it was mine and in my neighbourhood. I made seven dollars a month! I remember the proud exhilaration of riding my bike, fresh bag stuffed with the news of the entire world hanging off my hip. Was that a bad boast? Or was it head-held-high responsibility? Was it not the sense of starting to come fully alive and participating in the real world that I was feeling, even if it was only the block around my rural home?

Paul was boasting appropriately, but not beyond proper **limits** (Greek *ametros*—beyond what has been measured out). He was boasting only regarding the **area** (Greek *kanonos*—defined space, measuring standard, provincial boundaries) of service and influence God has **assigned** (Greek *meridzo*—shared, divided, distributed, or apportioned) to him. And this assignment has reached or extended even to the outer regions of Corinth.

Paul could take joyful, bold, and head-held-high responsibility for the areas of influential service God had assigned. He was not going beyond what God had given. He must live faithfully within the limits that Sovereign God had given and measured out (which in God's wisdom included Corinth but not Sparta, which was only one hundred kilometers away). Paul was seeking to please God in what had been apportioned to him and his team. He could boast—and should have—to the extent that he was faithfully being Christ's ambassador within the limits of the assignments God had uniquely given him. He couldn't answer for others, but he had to answer for what he did in the assignments entrusted to him, which included grumpy Corinthians.

The point is this: Sovereign God has sovereign assignments and areas of influence, measured and mapped out for his children and his church. This is how God has planned for his glory to fill the universe. Paul pointed to this reality in another of his letters: "He who descended [that is, God revealed in Jesus Christ] is the very one who ascended higher than all the heavens, in order to fill the whole universe" (Ephesians 4:10). Jesus came to earth embracing the limits of human flesh and time. He humbled himself to embrace the assignment of the cross and defeated sin and death. He rose from the dead as Lord and King of a new kingdom before whom every knee will someday bow. He ascended back to the heavens. This was planned in order to fill the whole universe with God's glory. And how would that glory be revealed? Through people. Through the church. Ephesians 4:1–16 calls the church to live its identity and calling in unity, utilizing the gifts Christ has given his people in order that the body of Christ might grow up and mature with each one of us doing the ambassadorial ministry assigned to us by Sovereign God. We are Christ's royal ambassadors with a royal assignment of reconciliation (2 Corinthians 5:20).

Our ambassadorial assignments are crucial because Christians are not free from the responsibilities or concerns of life in the world we inhabit.

Our Canadian family was once driving through San Francisco on our way north toward home when we were in a minor accident. Traffic had quickly come to a halt and I, the foreigner, rear-ended a car. No one was hurt, but there was some minor damage and we expected that no matter how quickly we drove north this would continue to be a responsibility we would not outrun. That proved true. A full year later, though we lived in Canada and far from that California street corner, what happened in downtown San Francisco remained a responsibility to care for.

It's somewhat like that for Christians. Our true identity is in Christ, and our true home is somewhere else, but we have responsibilities to tend to that we can't ignore, even if it does make us groan sometimes (2 Corinthians 5:4). Scripture is clear that we will need to answer for what we have done while in the limits of this body—whether good or bad (2 Corinthians 5:10). It is not out of fear, however, that we take our royal task seriously, but because this is God's world, and we are God's people. We live with an eternal perspective, so we care very much about living lives that please God now, because we know a new creation is coming. God will restore, set free, and recreate wherever we look. After all, God recreated us! God looked at us and saw not hopelessness, but the possibility of new creation and wholeness. God saw not an enemy to contend with, but the possibility of friendship and family. God saw his natural world aching because of sin and acted to awaken a Spirit-filled people to bring restoration (Romans 8:19). God acted in Christ to reconcile the world and it was costly. Now, stunningly, he has given to us the ministry of reconciliation (2 Corinthians 5:18). We are ambassadors of this other world, the kingdom of God, the shalom of God, which has broken into this world.

God is the Great Reconciler. We are the reconciled and now reconcilers. But what does this mean?

The Greek word *katallasso* was used for exchanging currency. To travel or immigrate to another country requires an exchange of currency. We can't use the dollars or pesos from the place we've left but need a new way of doing business. So, we reconcile—or *katallasso*—money, leaving behind one way of exchange for another. The word *katallasso* was also used for marriage. A couple leaves behind a previous reality for an entirely new one. Singleness is exchanged for marriage. The word was also used for when enemies become friends. They exchange enmity and bitterness, not just for armistice, tolerance, and a tentative truce, but for friendship.

Those who are now friends of God through Jesus Christ have been given the ministry or service (like the waiter of a table) of reconciliation. We serve a hungry world a new exchanged reality. Since we are spiritually at home with God in heaven because he has already reconciled us, we actively reconcile in our assignments in the world. The ministry of reconciliation is a precious gift we receive and steward. It is our act of obedience to Sovereign God, who is active in all places, in all times, seeking to draw people and creation back to himself. He has sent us and gifted us with a high ambassadorial charge! Christians aim to please God by doing the ministry of reconciliation in assignments God has given to help people be made friends with God, to find peace within themselves, to live at friendship with one another, and to care well for the world God has created.

So what are the assignments, areas, or spheres of influence God has given his ambassadors?

What happens when a child leaps into a puddle? There is a splash, waves and ripples. Your life has ripples of assignments—areas of influence and service—that Sovereign God has measured out. This is how you and I become part of God's grand plan to fill the universe with his glory as we march the parades of life.

*(Image by Shelley Simpson, 2022. Used with permission.)*

In the chapters that follow, we will wade through each of these ripples. We all have assignments that exist right now, not in the future, or when you graduate, and they don't expire with retirement. But before we jump in, here's a quick teaser:

- You (or the Greek word *ego)*—the fullness of who you are is your first assignment. Christians live in this beautiful mystery and purpose: "Those God foreknew he also predestined to be conformed to the image of his Son" (Romans 8:29).

- Creation (Greek *ktisis*, the product of God's speech)—the created world, geography, and topography you inhabit and even the smallest spot of dirt you can do something about.

- Your household (Greek *oikos*)—those closest to you that you have unique responsibility for.

- Your fellowship (Greek *koinonia*)—the community of believers God has given you discipleship and mission responsibility with.

- Your city or region (Greek *polis*)—the place you live, call home, and are not a tourist of or bystander in.

- Your nation or people (Greek *ethne*)—the nation state and people group you are part of.

- Your world (Greek *kosmos or ghay*)—the "ends of the earth" or "over there" that somehow has found a way into your heart and onto your radar.

We'll get our hands and hearts into the dirt of these assignments. We'll realize that no one is exempt or unnecessary in God's reconciling project. We'll come, I hope, to take joyfully and seriously the assignments in front of us, not looking somewhere else, but simply receiving the parade we're marching in. After all, everywhere you go, there you are.

Before we do that, however, we must answer important questions: What does God intend for us to do in our assignments? And what are we boastfully doing with our heads held high as ambassadors of Christ? As a blueprint for how we live within God's assignments, we return to 2 Corinthians 10. There, Paul described three activities he was living out in the areas of influence God had given him. These three apply to us as well:

We demolish strongholds opposed to God (2 Corinthians 10:3–6).

We build up people as ambassadors of Christ in their assignments (2 Corinthians 10:8).

We live in such a way as to be entrusted with more (2 Corinthians 10:15–16).

PHIL WAGLER

**We Demolish Strongholds Opposed to God.**

In our assignments, we are at war. But not with people. Christians are at war with spiritual strongholds that exist where we live and have been sent. These are the arguments and lofty opinions and pretensions that are raised up against the knowledge of God and his good purposes for creation.

In fact, because we have been given the same ministry of reconciliation that God himself is about (2 Corinthians 5:18), Christians have divine authority to destroy these strongholds to serve God in restoring four areas that human beings were created to experience wholeness in, but have been destroyed by sin and the spiritual powers of darkness: humanity's relationship with God, a person's peace with Self, people's unity and peace with others, and peace with the natural world. There is a spiritual dimension and a spiritual battle raging in each of these unreconciled areas.

We must see the world through spiritual eyes—with eyes of faith (2 Corinthians 5:1–10). We must see the possibility of new creation and spiritually engage the powers of darkness and evil that destroy what Sovereign God is seeking to do everywhere in order to undo the murderous schemes of the devil, who is focused on destroying God's good purposes—and particularly human beings made in God's image.

If we don't accept this spiritual task, we are vulnerable Christians. We will be blind and unaware and will easily trip up. This is where the spirituality of prayer, praise, being deeply rooted in Scripture, sabbath-keeping, fasting, and Christian community that discerns God's voice together are crucial. Demolishing strongholds, however, is only possible because Jesus Christ destroyed them on the cross and overcame them through his resurrection and ascension. Scripture says that "having disarmed the powers and authorities, he made a public spectacle of them, triumphing over them by the cross" (Colossians 2:15). If we are not reconciled to God through Jesus Christ, we remain slaves to sin and subjects of the kingdom of darkness and cannot share

32

God's ambassadorial authority. If we repent (which means to turn and go a different direction) of our complicity in darkness, then we receive the Spirit of God, which is power for salvation and authority over the schemes and tactics of Satan.

How do we join in the demolishing of strongholds Jesus accomplished?

**First, we join in the demolishing of strongholds by the authority that comes from friendship with the Father**. Jesus was always close with the Father. He tended that relationship above all others, even when the enemy tempted him to grab his assignment the wrong way. As redeemed and reconciled children of God, we are seated with Christ in his relationship of authority with the Father (Ephesians 2:6).

**Second, we join in the demolishing of strongholds by identifying the schemes of the devil.** Jesus encountered the demonic and commanded release for those who were captive. He engaged the real enemy even when speaking to people. His words rang true because they had a weight and authority from somewhere else and exposed the lies that bound people and the world. When we are clearly focused on the real enemy—Satan—and his strongholds, it changes how we pray, why we praise, and how we engage Christian community as we join Jesus's advance against the darkness that deceives the peoples, societies, and cultures assigned to us—and which we ourselves have been rescued from. Let us not forget, someone was fighting this battle on our behalf.

**Third, we join in the demolishing of strongholds with faithful love and self-giving humility.** In humility Jesus was obedient to death on the cross, and **this supreme act of love disarmed the power of evil.** The stronghold of sin and death came down as the Son of Man came serving and giving his life as a ransom for many. That same self-giving love and humility is the power of the kingdom of light in the face of the schemes of darkness.

So within our given assignments we ask: What strongholds need smashing here? And then we engage the spiritual battle Jesus's way to produce the lasting fruit of heaven that Jesus has chosen and sent us to produce.

## We Build Up People.

Paul was clear that he was boasting a bit about the authority he had—and we all have—in Christ to demolish deceptive strongholds. But that authority used to battle spiritual darkness is utilized much differently with people. With people, we use divine authority not to destroy but to build up. Again, this is done Jesus's way. So how did Jesus build up people?

He came to set captives free and bring good news to the poor. He extended mercy to those who were deemed unworthy of it. He embraced outcasts, ate with the despised, saw tax collectors in trees, and healed bleeding women in crowds and blind men on the roadside. He brought into his circle those who were enemies with one another, uniting the most unlikely and equipping them to do the will of God in the world. He sought to free people from the snare of wealth. He forgave the offense of sin. He called people to repentance and a new course of life, inviting them to walk away from sin because the love and mercy of God had appeared. He gave people the Holy Spirit to live a life of power with the authority to build up as he built up.

This is what Paul was saying to the Corinthians that applies to us: the authority he has is that *same* authority Jesus came with. This is the *same* authority Paul experienced in his own life, having turned from being a terrorist and persecutor who destroyed people into a servant who built up people as an ambassador of Christ. Sometimes that authority means comfort and encouragement. Sometimes it requires heart-to-heart honesty. At all times, we are servants building up those predestined to be conformed to the image of Christ (Romans 8:29). We are all meant to be more and more like Jesus.

So within our given assignments, we ask: What will build up people in Christ here?

We ask this recognizing that as part of the body of Christ—his church—we are simultaneously part of two different communities. First, we are a theological community that is an eternal, spiritual family. In this moment we are the generation who are custodians of memory. To us has been passed God's family story, the gospel. We are theologians interpreting contemporary history that is still being made in light of the revelation of God in Jesus Christ. We build up by taking seriously this task to care for God's good news. We know, preserve, interpret, and live God's good news in our time. We are to ensure it is passed on to the next generation.

Second, we are part of a missionary community that is a contemporary, contextual community. We are those responsible to communicate God's revelation of Jesus Christ here and now, in this place and among our people. We translate the truth of Jesus and the kingdom of God in proclamation and demonstration. We verbally and visibly interpret God's ways into our time. We are missionaries in the places and among the peoples where Sovereign God has placed us. So we build people up by growing our discipleship through a deeper theological life (a life that knows God, not just knows about him) so we can together steward the gospel for this age. And we build up by taking seriously our identity as those sent as missionaries to our time where the ways of Jesus and his kingdom must be proclaimed and demonstrated.

**We Live in Such a Way as to Be Entrusted with More.**
Paul accepted that the Corinthians—though they had been somewhat difficult—were his God-given assignment. He was not concerned about what others are doing because this was clear: the grumpy and divisive Corinthians were his God-given charge.

Paul's faithfulness to God was evidenced in the maturity of the Corinthians. And as they matured, he expected an overflow because the strongholds had fallen, they were built up in Christ, and they had become fit for God's expanding holy assignments. The aroma of Christ in Corinth would be caught by the currents and carried to other places.

This would influence individuals, households, the city, and even the Roman Empire. As the Corinthians matured, Paul knew God would open new opportunities for him. Paul had dreams beyond Corinth, but he accepted that new assignments would be the result of growth in the Corinthians and himself. Faithfulness, not selfish ambition, was the task at hand. God entrusts more responsibility and influence to those who are responsible and faithful.

Jesus said his disciples would do greater works then he because he was going to the Father, and the Spirit was coming (John 14:12). We are tasked to these greater works as ministers of reconciliation: demolishing strongholds, building up people, and contributing to maturity and God's shalom. We serve to bring heaven's aroma and influence in the parade marked out for us, in hopes that God gives opportunity for more. Like Jesus and Paul, we expect more, but not at the expense of what is right in front of us. We focus on the maturing, Christlike, and Shalom-yielding reality with whomever and wherever Sovereign God has chosen to put us.

God gives more to those who are faithful with a little. God gives new assignments—possibly even expanded assignments—to those who produce maturity. The genuine ambassadors of Christ are the ones commended for their faithfulness. Faithful ambassadors are entrusted with more.

Faithful ambassadors do not chase fame, celebrity, power, or money; nor do they demand their own rights. All of these are heinous and deceptive strongholds that can trap and discredit. Influence in God's kingdom is Christlike character and servanthood. In a world increasingly relying on influencers and protesters, God looks for the influence of faithful servanthood. God is not searching for those with the best YouTube videos or Instagram posts, or even the biggest vision, but those who tend faithfully and obediently the assignment in front of them.

So within our assignments, we ask: Am I living here in such a way that I could be entrusted with more?

To summarize, Christians are reconciled to God in Christ and called to be ministers of reconciliation: the ambassadors of Christ. We are the aroma of Christ in a small-town parade God has chosen, resting in the limits and areas of influence Sovereign God has mapped out. And in every rippling assignment Sovereign God has given us, we're holding our heads high as we do three things:

- Demolish strongholds that are destroying God's purposes and people made in his image.

- Build up people in Christ so they can step into their own assignments with ambassadorial authority.

- Live in such a way that we can be entrusted with more of God's ambassadorial tasks in order that his glory increasingly fills the universe.

# CHAPTER 3:

## YOU ARE THE ASSIGNMENT

Viola Desmond's likeness adorns Canada's new ten-dollar bill. Her unlikely rise to such prominence began in a movie theatre and because of a one-cent tax. On November 8, 1946, Desmond, an entrepreneur with her own cosmetic company, was on a business trip when her car broke down. The car couldn't be repaired until the next day, so to pass the time she went to see a movie in New Glasgow, Nova Scotia. Though segregation was not provincial law, this theatre expected white patrons to sit in the lower seats for forty cents and black patrons to be in the balcony for thirty cents. The tax difference was one measly cent.

Viola didn't know about this local discrimination, so she decided to move to the lower seats because she was nearsighted and could see better. She was asked to move but refused, offering to pay the difference in price. That was rejected, and she was arrested for a tax violation. Viola Desmond spent the next twelve hours in jail and had to pay a $20 tax evasion fine because of an unpaid one-cent tax. The injustice eventually ended up in court with the government winning that legal battle over one cent in tax while not acknowledging the clear discrimination that caused the whole mess in the first place. This lamentable injustice is why Viola Desmond's likeness was chosen for the Canadian ten-dollar bill.

Despite Viola's beautiful face adorning Canada's violet currency, we know this is not Viola Desmond's money. Who does the ten-dollar bill belong to? Truth is, even if it's in our hand, it doesn't belong to us. Even if ten dollars is passed around, shoved in pockets, given to charity, or blown on a ten-year old's sugar rampage through a convenience store and then recirculated and used for a drug deal, of all things, in reality the piece of plasticized paper belongs to the Bank of Canada, which has the power to buy, print, and control it. In the end, we can leave to the Bank of Canada what belongs to the Bank of Canada, for it is the simple and courageous humanity of Viola Desmond that legitimizes her worthiness to be memorialized as she now is. After all, it is who we are that is of ultimate worth.

Sovereign God has given us life assignments.

We are plopped into the puddle of life and discover that God has given gifts, personalities, and limits that we are to surrender to our maker for his choosing so that his glory might fill the universe. Remember, Jesus said to his first disciples, "You did not choose me, but I chose you and appointed you so that you might go and bear fruit—fruit that will last" (John 15:16). God's purpose is that we produce the fruit of his good kingdom in his world, in the days we have breath, and within the limits set for us.

This all starts with you! You are the first assignment God has given you. Everything we experience hinges greatly on what every person does with the life given to them. "What do I do with me?" is a loaded question we can skip past as we frolic through life, focusing on what should be done by or about others! The Lord's words to Ezekiel the prophet are for us too: "Son of man, listen carefully and take to heart all the words I speak to you" (Ezekiel 3:10).

Isn't it amazing how quickly children (and adults) deflect responsibility for their own actions? "It wasn't me!" "Did you see what they did?" One of our children conveniently reasoned that Jesus's words "do to others what you would have them do to you" (Matthew 7:12) always began with the other person. Conveniently therefore, if your sibling hit you, then they wanted you to hit them. Jesus of course was saying something much more difficult. He said the law and prophets are summed up in me beginning with myself and acting as I would want you to do to me. If I start with me, I am forced to deal with my actions, my self, my soul first. I must examine my pride, arrogance, and sinfulness. I am forced to die to myself to do to you what I would want you to die to yourself to do to me. God always starts with me.

I am an only child. The burden of only kids is that they can never say, "But she ... but he ... they made me do it!" That doesn't work, because it's obviously you! In a sense our good heavenly Father looks upon each of us as if we were his only child. Even more, before being reconciled to God, we are orphans, separated from our true home. Despite this, God the creator of the universe sees, knows, and pursues us! In C.S. Lewis's marvelous book, *The Horse and His Boy*, Aslan the Lion speaks to confused and discouraged Shasta, who is wondering about his friend Aravis, and says, "Child, I am telling you your story, not hers. No one is told any story but their own."[2] And so our first assignment we need to live with is perhaps the most difficult of all: ourselves as orphaned only children in a great big, complex world.

One night, living near the US border, I crossed over to buy gas and milk (it was cheaper for our growing family to do this). This time I only had cash with me. When I went to pay the cashier, however, I ended up a bit short on US dollars. I did, however, have enough Canadian dollars to make up the difference. When I proposed this plan to the bearded, tattooed, "just-doing-my-job" gas station attendant, he literally laughed! "Uh, no! We can't take that," he said. So I had to

---

[2] C.S. Lewis, *The Horse and His Boy* (London: Fontana, 1954), 139.

put milk back and live with it. I could have argued, "Listen, I've got hundreds, even thousands of these beautifully coloured notes that the Bank of Canada endorses to my name," but it wouldn't have mattered. This gruff, minimum-wage employee had every right to overrule my abundance, even the authority of the Bank of Canada, and even the British monarch by saying, "That is basically worthless here. I can't take it."

In Matthew 21–22 a fascinating series of events flows toward a conversation about money. Matthew 21 begins with Jesus riding into Jerusalem. He was the Messiah, the humble king promised by the prophet Zechariah, welcomed by his joyous subjects. His arrival was not what they expect, however. He came with a hopeful authority that produced joyful praise in the crowds but disturbed those in authority, who were convinced they knew how God and the world worked.

In the temple courts, Jesus was asked by what authority he was acting and teaching. Why should they receive him? After all he was just a small-town rabbi from Nazareth, of all places (21:23–27). The fundamental emerging question was, who has authority? Who gets to have the say over us? In response, Jesus asked a question about the baptism John the Baptist had been performing. "Was it from heaven, or of human origin?" he asked (21:25). Every Gospel tells of John the Baptist baptizing people who were repenting of sin, of life on their own terms, and coming under the authority of God. John's baptism wasn't just a wilderness spiritual experience but called for life-altering action. John called people to come under God's authority and start acting like it in everyday life. "Produce fruit in keeping with repentance," he charged (Matthew 3:8). If you have more than you need, share. Don't take advantage of others in your work. Be content with your pay. Stop demanding more at the expense of others (Luke 3:11–14). John pointed away from himself to the coming Messiah, who would fill people with the fire of the Holy Spirit, making the power and ways of God very personal and socially impactful.

So when Jesus asked about whether John's baptism came with divine authority, he was getting very personal and challenging the social landscape. And his detractors knew it! So to get around the question of authority, which would have required assessment of whether they were under their own authority, the authority of a religious tradition, or authority that was granted and tolerated by the Roman Empire, they chose convenient ignorance: "We don't know" (21:27). Jesus, playing by their game, then refused to answer their question as well.

The issue is authority. Will human beings, even religious human beings, receive what God is doing in Jesus Christ? Will we accept the revealed authority of God, or won't we? Who will rule me? Oh, what will I do with me?

Those running to John's baptism were saying "We're done with other rulers. We're coming back to Yahweh. We want to know how to live and whose voice to ultimately listen to." The chief priests and religious leaders, on the other hand, weren't sure.

In Matthew 21, three parables follow this stalemate over authority. In each one, Jesus elevated the call to bring one's life under the authority of Sovereign God revealed in him, the humble King Messiah. In the parable of the two sons (21:28–32), the righteous son is the one who does what the Father asks, not just the one who talks about it. In the parable of the tenants (21:33–46), the workers in the vineyard reject the son sent by the owner of the vineyard and refuse to produce the fruit of the kingdom. In the parable of the wedding banquet (22:1–14), guests are invited to a royal wedding, but they all make very personal, reasoned excuses and reject the authority of the master of the party. Jesus was driving home a point: God is personally revealing himself to those who even hold the promises of the Hebrew Scriptures, yet they refuse to come under God's authority revealed in the Messiah. True allegiance is revealed not in words but in action. At issue is not whether we can quote Scripture or have positional authority, but whether we obey God's voice and live in joyful surrender to the authority of the King of kings.

All this leads to a trap set for Jesus (Matthew 22:15–22). The Pharisees (a religious political party who wanted to preserve obedience to the law of God) came with the Herodians (a political party loyal to the dynasty of King Herod; the same Herod who had the babies killed in Bethlehem). The Herodians saw supporting the royal family as the last hope of retaining for the Jews a fragment of national government that could embody Jewish values and traditions. This was the only way, they believed, to avoid absolute dependence upon Rome. Since the family of Herod only held their power by the will of the Roman emperor, paying tribute to the supreme power of Caesar was deemed a small price to pay. This desire to hold on to power and self-preservation was blinding God's chosen people. The Jews were to be a different people among all peoples of the earth, through whom a Messiah would come for all peoples. This Messiah now stood among them asking all to come to the party. But Jesus, the unlikely donkey-riding king with his message of the transforming authority of God, was wrecking their plans and getting too personal. He needed to be dealt with. So they set a trap.

They asked about taxes. "Is it right to pay the imperial tax to Caesar or not?" (22:17). If Jesus said no, they could hand him over to Rome as an insurrectionist. If he said yes, they would have him on their side and could use his fame to enhance their cause. Jesus saw this as evil. The question exposed these leaders. They were not interested in bearing the fruit of God's kingdom at all but wanted to preserve life on their own terms. They wanted to write history their way.

Jesus asked to see a coin. A denarius was put in front of him (the equivalent of about a day's pay). "Whose image is on this?" he asked. The answer was obvious, "It's Caesar."

"So," reasoned Jesus, "give back to Caesar what is Caesar's, and to God what is God's" (22:21). Jaws dropped. There was silence. Why?

What had Jesus just done? He had put his finger on the main question confronting not just first-century Jews in a complex world, but every human being: Whose am I? To whom will I give authority? Which authority will I serve? After all, who bears the image of God?

Every Jew knew that God created human beings male and female in God's image (Genesis 1:26–28). So go ahead and give to Caesar the scrap of metal with his image on it, which is worth something more or something less depending on which way the wind blows. Go ahead and fight and claw to hold on to some semblance of power and privilege. Go ahead and make your primary assignment figuring out how to serve the authority of Rome, which will take and take from you; destroying your soul, demanding your allegiance, dividing you from others, and seeking to rule you (no matter how loudly you scream that God is who you serve).

The piercing question is, have I given God me?

This is Jesus's question, "Will you receive me, the Messiah, God revealed in human flesh, through whom all things were created, for whom all things are created, and who holds all things together, as Lord and Leader of life?"

Is God my authority? And if not, who or what is?

Recall these words: "All this is from God, who reconciled us to himself through Christ and gave us the ministry of reconciliation" (2 Corinthians 5:18). Once again, "reconciled" in Greek is *katallasso*. It was originally used for exchanging money from one currency to another. Christians have been exchanged, reconciled to God through Christ, transformed from wandering orphans, set free from the grip of sin and death, and adopted with a new identity as God's children and heirs and are now friends of the King eternal! A Christian is a new reality in the world, a different currency. We have come under a new authority and have a new purpose. To be Christian is to become God's currency so you can bear the fruit of his kingdom in your God-given assignments. A Christian is the currency of God's transaction and interaction in the world!

This brings us to the tasks God has given us in the assignment of me.

The first is to demolish strongholds. We ask, what strongholds need smashing here? Since you are the first assignment God has given you, you must ask diligently, "What strongholds need smashing in me?" The Holy Spirit, if you have ears to hear, will expose strongholds, divided loyalties, and the duplicitous, double agent life you may be living. The Spirit of God will ask for a great exchange. Like the Herodians and Pharisees, we all come with allegiances to authorities we may be blind to or sold out to. We will probably be offended when God pokes the idols we have given authority to and unwittingly serve: A brand of politics or ideology; wealth or pleasure; impurity or lust; a podcaster or author; an identity, a wound, a trauma, or victimhood; an ethnicity or people group; or the authority of the self that demands what I want or "my truth."

These allegiances become strongholds. We will obey what they say before we obey the creator. This surrendering of our dignity to lesser things is the surrendering of our first assignment. We give ourselves to Caesar. Jesus's command is to give God what is God's. And we are the image and likeness of God. If my first assignment is me, then I must first ask whose authority I have given myself to. And who has true authority over me will show up in how I live, what I represent, how I spend money, energy, and time, how I approach suffering, the community I seek, who I am under pressure, whose voice I live by, and—as we will shortly see—how I love. Will I truly seek my Father's will to be done? Will Jesus be Lord of all of me? Will the Holy Spirit be free to transform me increasingly into the image of Christ, that I may bear his fruit in the assignments God has given?

It all starts here.

There is a battle raging for my allegiance, a battle over strongholds, and in the cross of Christ those strongholds have come tumbling down.

When Jesus held that coin, he was smashing strongholds and getting very personal. I must ask what strongholds need smashing. I must be ready to confess and turn from them. I may need the help of others—a pastor, a discipleship group, perhaps even a counselor. I will need to practice spiritual disciplines, being grounded in Scripture, prayer, spiritual community, fasting, and sabbath rest. This battle is real, and it is in me, over me, for me, and in Christ has already been won. In the assignment of you, you must now live this victory.

Our second task in the assignment of you is to build up people. We ask, "What will build up people in Christ here?"

How do we build ourselves up? After all, as those dead in our trespasses and sins, we must first be raised up from spiritual death by the power of God. We're orphans without a home. Before we can be built up, we need to be raised up to new life. We need to be born a second time (John 3:3, 7). This is God's work. Our building up, ironically, begins in dying. Only in dying to self and a full-surrender sacrifice are we born into a new understanding of life and purpose. If we come under the authority of God, we come alive as we receive His words as authoritative to build us up.

In Matthew 16, Jesus asked his disciples who they would say he was. Peter responded, "You are the Messiah, the Son of the Living God" (16:16). This is *the* coming-under-authority declaration and confession. This is the confession, Jesus said, upon which he would build his church, against which the gates of hell would not stand. Jesus countered any idea the disciples might have that he would do what the Herodians were hoping for—building up a political haven for Jews in a baffling world. Jesus said that though he was God with us and worthy of full allegiance, he would be rejected, killed, and resurrected. Peter put on the brakes, "No chance! This can't happen!" Jesus gave an immediate rebuke, "Get behind me, Satan! You are tripping up the way the kingdom of God must come and be built up. Your thinking is too human and warped by split allegiances" (see 16:22–23). And he pushed further: "Whoever wants to be my disciple must deny themselves and take up their cross and follow me. For whoever wants to save their life will lose it, but whoever loses their life for me will find it" (Matthew 16:24–25).

To build up requires tearing down. To be built up into my assignment requires an ongoing dying and surrender of myself to God whose humble authority I have submitted to. To be built up requires seeking to please God first in every aspect of life. But happily, this is not a burden like serving the authorities and strongholds of Caesar and their ilk. Hitching to Jesus's yoke is easy and light (Matthew 11:30), but not cheap. We take up a cross, but it is in response to the God of love.

When cornered by a lawyer and asked, "Which is the greatest commandment in the law?" (Matthew 22:36), Jesus was clear: "'Love the Lord your God with all your heart and with all your soul and with all your mind.' This is the first and greatest commandment. And the second is like it: 'Love your neighbor as yourself.' All the Law and the Prophets hang on these two commandments" (Matthew 22:37–40). Loving God with all I am—heart, soul, and mind (and in Mark's Gospel "strength" is added)—and loving my neighbour *as myself* is the way the revelation of God holds together. Jesus embodied this. He loved the Father with all he was, up to and including the cross. He loved his neighbour, even his enemies. And this was the supreme witness of love for self—he was doing to others as he would have them to do him! So when Jesus said, "Take up your cross and follow me," he was saying, "Love and live in the way I love and live and even die, for in this way you are expressing the deep awareness that you are loved unconditionally and unreservedly by God." Jesus's supreme invitation is to understand that allegiance to God is not about rule-keeping but love so dynamic and alive that it will die to remain true. This opens the way for us to live in all our assignments as transformative ambassadors of the reconciling and other-worldly love of God.

Remember Peter?

He who spoke so boldly eventually failed miserably. He denied knowing Jesus in the Lord's most desperate hour. He was selfish and love-less. He surrendered to the authority of security and self-preservation when Jesus was on trial. After the resurrection, Peter was unsure where he fit in the grand adventure that King Jesus would lead. Had Peter become useless? Could he love himself? Jesus took Peter for a little walk (John 21). Jesus didn't fire or even correct Peter with a condescending "I told you so." Instead, he asked—three times—a more challenging question: "Do you love me?" (John 21:15–17). Peter's rebuilding began with love. This is key question Jesus still asks despite our mistakes, capitulations, denials, and failures: Do you love me? Do you love the Lord your God with all you are? Do you love your neighbour? Do you love yourself?

The opposite of love for self is not self-hatred but self-worship. It is the ultimate in self-denigration for a person made in God's image to give allegiance and authority to a narrative and voice that are not the creator's, and we are not God. God's voice to us is always and forever "I love you." God's love invites worship. Self-worship undermines love for God and ironically leaves us not even loving ourselves. Self-worship is unsustainable, dishonest, and self-destructive. Self-worship literally destroys because our own voice is not a large enough authority and is often our own worst enemy. This is why Jesus calls us to take up our cross and die to ourselves, for in dying to self we are freed from the tyrannical master that is the God-less self, deceived by Satan.

In dying to self, I discover love and life and am raised up as a new creation, secure as a beloved child of God, a friend of God, filled with the Spirit of God, empowered for life in this body and moment, within the limits Sovereign God sets, as an ambassador of Christ's reconciling, resurrected ways. From the wonder of this new position, we stand amazed by the loving mercy and kindness of God in Christ and, in response, offer our limited lives as a living sacrifice, holy and pleasing to God (Romans 12:1–2). Worship is life given over to God in response to the love of God. Worship is life lived as love for God.

The apostle Paul described how he built himself up: "I have been crucified with Christ and I no longer live, but Christ lives in me. The life I now live in the body, I live by faith in the Son of God, who loved me and gave himself for me" (Galatians 2:20). He took up his cross because he was loved. And his love for God was expressed with the limited body, lifetime, and assignments God had given him.

Love of God. Love of neighbour. Love of self. These are not compartmentalized in Scripture; they are one, just as God is One. When we experience the love of God and love God with all we are, we will love our neighbours as we have come to love ourselves. We will be built up as bearers of the image of God. This is how God will fill the universe with his glory. To build yourself up in the assignment of you requires a soul-searching answer to this question: Is my life built up by, defined by, reshaped by, and compelled by love for God because I know the love of God revealed in Jesus Christ?

This is why Jesus turned to Peter—who was still trying to come to grips with the depth and power of resurrecting love in the shadow of his failure, weakness, and limitations—and poignantly said, "Follow me" (John 21:19, 22). Peter, comparing himself to others who did not make his mistakes, responded as we might: "Well, what about him, or her, what about these other kids and all their issues?" Jesus simply invited Peter to the freedom of accepting limits: *They are not your first assignment, Peter. You are the assignment. Child, I am telling you your story, not theirs. No one is told any story but their own.* "You, follow me" (John 21:22).

All of our assignments begin with this question: Have I given God me? Have I demolished and come out from under binding strongholds? Have I died to myself and now love God with all that I am? Am I being built up and raised up as an ambassador for Christ? Will I follow where he leads? And as we come to our third task in this assignment, am I here and now obedient to the voice of the good shepherd in such a way that I could be entrusted with more? Contrary to our expectations and pursuits, being entrusted with more does not first begin with gifts, talents, personality, intellect, or reputation. Every biblical character who stepped into their assignments—like Moses, Esther, Isaiah, Mary, and Peter—felt unqualified, disqualified, and unworthy. But God wasn't first interested in those things. The lasting fruit of God's kingdom always began—and would grow in beauty and influence—to the extent that they followed him and obeyed his voice.

Which leads us to a sobering reality. We can say, "I've given me over to God." We can say, "I die to myself and love you, God!" But if we don't follow him and obey his voice when God challenges our wrong allegiances, sin, or the lies we believe; if we do not abide in love, know his ways, and become more and more like him, he cannot and will not entrust us with more. God longs to entrust his ambassadors with more and greater responsibility. More of Jesus is needed. It is what creation needs. It is what your household, your fellowship, your city, your nation, and the whole wide world needs. And it all begins with the assignment that is you.

Give to God what is God's.

## QUESTIONS FOR THIS ASSIGNMENT

- Are there any personal strongholds standing in the way of giving God you?

- What personal traumas, struggles, habits, or realities need to be addressed to build you up as God desires for you?

- How are you comparing yourself to others in a way that is hindering your own joyful surrender to the purposes and wholeness of God in your life?

- What would you point to that would indicate that you could, or should not, be entrusted with more?

# CHAPTER 4
## CREATION IS YOUR ASSIGNMENT

We are plopped into the puddle of life and discover that God has given gifts, personalities and limits that we are to surrender to our maker in order that his glory might fill the universe. Jesus said to the first disciples, "You did not choose me, but I chose you and appointed you so that you might go and bear fruit—fruit that will last" (John 15:16). In every ripple of our assignments God intends that we first be reconciled to himself through Jesus Christ and filled with his Spirit in order that we might serve as a representation of God himself. We are ambassadors of Christ. We are the demonstration of a whole new reconciled way of living. Our first assignment is to give to God what is God's, our very selves made in God's image. Our next assignment, naturally, is creation.

As a young child I spent much time on my grandparents' small farm. The barn, with its weathered boards, stood atop a hill looking down over the winding river that flowed beside my small hometown. I loved going there. Morning and night my grandparents milked about a dozen cows. I can still hear the rumble of the milk separator rattling away as it separated the rich cream from the fresh milk, drawing the attention of fat barn cats. I especially favoured one brown cow named Bossy. She was a gentle giant. Quite uncommon for bovines, she would allow us to ride her like a horse. I recall being lifted and placed on her wide, warm back, my little legs straddling this large beast that could have tossed and trampled me. I loved her, and so did my grandparents. They loved all the creatures God had entrusted to them—sheep, cattle, chickens, the border collie, the cats, the pigs—along with the large garden just across the gravel lane from the barn, the crab-apple trees they pruned so my grandma could preserve cinnamon crab-apples every year, and that slow-moving river where we fished.

Speaking of fish …

The Old Testament story of Jonah takes place in the eighth century BC and is known mostly for what happens in the middle of it when a large fish swallows the prophet of the Lord as he runs from his assignment. The big fish spits Jonah out—happy to get rid of him, it seems—when the rogue prophet finally gets serious with God and agrees that delivering the Ninevites a message of repentance and grace in the face of impending doom is better than hot-tubbing in aquatic stomach acid. Jonah finally goes to Nineveh, the capital city of the Assyrian Empire that for centuries had subdued nations and was now threatening Jonah's Jewish people.

God had given Jonah a clear and difficult assignment. It's understandable that Jonah sought to get out of it. But when he finally obeyed, the Ninevites believed and changed course. In fact, the king called for a massive show of national repentance, calling everyone to humility before God, who is referred to by the Hebrew name *Elohim* (the Supreme God), the name given to God in the opening words of Scripture: "In the beginning God created the heavens and the earth" (Genesis 1:1).

The king of Assyria also decreed that not only the people, but even the animals were to be covered in sackcloth (an ancient sign of repentance), call out to God, and turn from their evil and violence (Jonah 3:8). The king accepted that every single creature in Nineveh was complicit and unified in selfishness, evil, and violence and that *Elohim* had spit someone in their general direction to offer a lifeline. The political center of a world empire humbled itself entirely. God saw this humility and loved it and relented from bringing disaster (3:10).

Lest we think the king's yanking of the Ninevite beasts into all this is just silly, the book of Jonah includes a cornucopia of creation enveloped in the mess of the world *and* the marvel of transformation. It's as if all creation is longing for things to change! The account includes plenty of human beings created to be God's representation of himself, from Jonah the reluctant prophet to Assyrians rich and poor. Jonah knew of God's mercy and kindness and desire to have his shalom-wholeness and peace be the way of all peoples, but he ran *from* God.

The Ninevites were given to evil and violence, but they ran *to* God. The prophet who knows the Lord and the Ninevites who don't know are both sometimes right and wrong. Beyond humanity the story also includes the wind, the sea, and that big fish utilized to get Jonah's attention. After the Ninevites softened their hearts—which was an inconvenient truth to Jonah, who wanted to see the destruction of his enemies—the LORD used a plant (the Hebrew word is quite specific, most likely referring to the castor-oil plant that grows fast and large) as an object lesson. A worm ate the plant. A strong east wind blew and the blazing sun beat down upon him. Creation was groaning in unison to get the attention of the Ninevites and Jonah! The natural world was bellowing as Psalm 19:3–4 declares:

> "They have no speech, they use no words; no sound is heard from them.
>
> Yet their voice goes out into all the earth, their words to the ends of the world."

The Ninevites eventually humbled themselves before God's special revelation, his specific word of good news for all people through the prophet. But we don't know if Jonah humbled himself. The book ends with Jonah saying that he's so angry with how this all turned out that he wants to die (4:9). But the Lord gets the last word: "You have been concerned about this plant, though you did not tend it or make it grow. It sprang up overnight and died overnight. And should I not have concern for the great city of Nineveh, in which there are more than a hundred and twenty thousand people who cannot tell their right hand from their left—and also many animals?" (Jonah 4:10–11).

The plant exposed Jonah's selfish, stubborn heart and calcified thinking. He didn't care about the plant because it was a marvel of God's good creation. He only loved the shade it gave him. The simple plant revealed a complex sickness in the prophet's soul. He was self-centered (the plant was for him), he was ethno-centered (God was for only *his* people), and he was full of schadenfreude (the German word for the pleasure or self-satisfaction that comes from learning of or witnessing the troubles, failures, or humiliation of others). Jonah didn't want God to be for all creation, just his part of it.

More than a cute kid's story, the account of Jonah reveals the Lord compassionately concerned for and unapologetically involving the whole of his creation for his glory in the world. God was responding to the groaning of creation, the cry for a different way, and the question hangs in the hot sun: would those who know the Lord care the way he does?

We must consider the impact we who humble ourselves like Ninevites before the undeserved grace and kindness of God are to have as new creations in the world belonging to our creator. Romans 8 describes the life we are given when we give ourselves to God and become vessels of the Spirit of God. In Christ we are new creations, free from condemnation, and filled by the breath of God, to live led by the Spirit of God. To be God's children is to call God our Father and be wrapped in his arms of love. It also means we wrap our arms around all his ways and wonders. We become like little kids loving the rich, smelly, and earthy wonder of the farm.

The apostle Paul wrote, "The creation waits in eager expectation for the children of God to be revealed. For the creation was subjected to frustration, not by its own choice, but by the will of the one who subjected it, in hope that the creation itself will be liberated from its bondage to decay and brought into the freedom and glory of the children of God" (Romans 8:19–21).

Creation groans to get our attention. The storm at sea screamed at Jonah to wake up to his assignment because evil and violence were destroying those made in God's image! When human beings awaken to the love of God in Christ and take seriously our first assignment, then creation and humanity can begin to realize the fullness of what God intended when his love created both in the first place. From that first assignment we step into the second assignment: creation. We can be the children of God creation is groaning for.

Which takes us back to the beginning. Christian theology begins with God as creator. God's salvation—and his sending of Jesus to save the whole world from sin—is only understood rightly when we begin with God as creator. Scripture begins with "In the beginning God created the heavens and the earth. Now the earth was formless and empty, darkness was over the surface of the deep, and the Spirit of God was hovering over the waters." (Genesis 1:1–2). The story of Jonah is rooted here. Why would God bother about violent Ninevites and their animals and use wind, fish, and plants to accomplish his purposes? Because God created them. They are his. He is seeking the wholeness, well-being, redemption, restoration—what the Hebrew scriptures call *shalom*—of his entire creation. This is our Father's world.

Psalm 24:1–2 sings,

"The earth is the LORD's, and everything in it, the world, and all who live in it;

for he founded it on the seas and established it on the waters."

This passage shaped the sense and scope of mission for Anabaptist Christians in the sixteenth century, who had no power or privilege yet believed they were to be involved in taking the good news of Jesus Christ to the ends of the earth in a way that cared for the whole earth. Christian mission is not just about the detached souls, but the entirety of the created order because the earth is the Lord's and everything in it! Christian mission must be interested in the wholeness of creation and humanity's interaction with it.

The Society for the Prevention of Cruelty to Animals (SPCA), for instance, was birthed not out of a veterinary college or Earth Day movement, but from the biblical vision of William Wilberforce, who gave his entire political career as a British Member of Parliament to see the African slave trade abolished. He saw his Christian faith as applicable in the freedom of enslaved human beings as in the horrendous treatment of animals. Even Earth Day itself—marked globally on April 22—was founded not by Greenpeace but by a Pentecostal Christian named John McConnell, who dug deep into a biblical theology of God the creator.

A biblical theology of creation care follows this logic (as described by John Copeland Nagle in *Christianity and Human Rights*[3]):

- **God created the world.** Which is why rejecting a creator God in society will not help but eventually hinder any environmental movement, for it will not lead to wholeness and shalom but to evil and violence. It's also why Christians

---

[3] Thomas Schirrmacher and Thomas K. Johnson, *Creation Care and Loving Our Neighbors* (Bonn: Culture and Science Publishing, 2018), 25.

who believe in Creator God but reject the care of the earth—the limited sphere of God's unique activity in the universe—dishonour the creator.

• **God pronounced the creation to be good.** We cannot say the earth doesn't matter because it will all decay or just consume it for selfish purposes. Such use of God's creation is ultimately not good. Neither, however, can we say creation is good without a creator, for its goodness is tied to the inherent goodness of the one who spoke it into existence.

• **God is the owner of all creation.** It never belongs to us. Even property we might "own" is the Lord's.

• **God gave humanity dominion over creation.** Humanity is God's representation in the world. It was Sovereign God's sovereign choice to put creation in our hands. We are of immeasurable dignity and worth, and our creator sets us apart for the high call of ruling, stewarding, and tending what he has made. Our stewardship of creation is to draw out what will contribute to goodness and well-being. We are not subordinate to creation. We do not serve creation. We serve God by tending what God has made for his glory. When humanity surrenders its assignment to have dominion—to act like God's representatives—creation itself will groan and convulse to remind us to take back our God given dignity and assignment. It is notable that indigenous cultures around the world have an intimate and mutual relationship with creation and place a high value on stewardship. The industrializing and commodifying of creation—a modern corruption of the "dominion" mandate—fundamentally changed humanity's participation with the created world. There is much to learn about being God's representatives in creation from indigenous and ancient paths.

• **God charged us with the responsibility of caring for creation.** "The LORD God took the man and put him in the Garden of Eden to work it and take care of it" (Genesis 2:15). We work and care. We shovel and feed. Our sweat, our talents, even the development of technologies, are not to destroy the earth but to carefully maximize the endless potential God has deposited in his creation for goodness to flourish for everyone and everything. Work—as God designed it—is not for us, but for God and the common good in our spheres of influence. Care—as God designed it—is not for the filling of our bank accounts, but for God and the common good in our spheres of influence. God has given us an assignment in the created world. My perspiration and abilities, no matter my age, whether I am in a wheelchair or able-bodied, vinedresser or CEO, are to be given to the responsibilities of work and care.

• **God alone is worthy of worship.** We never worship creation, for that becomes idolatry and deception and the surrender of our true dignity. Idolatry subjugates human beings to that which we were to tend and have dominion over and results in a disparaging of humanity. I once followed a vehicle through my city with a bumper sticker reading: "Dogs: because humans suck!" It's cheeky but reveals a fundamental reversal of the creator's plan. After all, the dog is only as wonderful as its owner, and its owner is only wonderful when taking their created God-given dignity seriously. We don't worship nature, but neither do we serve ourselves. We do not do as we want, raping and pillaging as if we are gods and goddesses. We worship God. We are the sons and daughters of God honouring our good creator as we tend to the groaning of creation, seeking to restore even the smallest piece of dirt we have been given responsibility for. Our work and care are acts of worship as we give God what is worthy of him.

• **Creation has suffered the effects of the entry of sin into the world.** This is why you must be the first assignment. Creation groans because of us. It was human rebellion against the creator, against our own identity and assignment, that forced creation's groan. We need to get right and give ourselves again to God in humility and repentance. This does not mean, however, that humanity is the problem. Some ideologies imply that if humanity would just go away, the natural world would be saved.

But the problem is not humanity; the problem is sin. Sin must be destroyed, and that's what Christ did! When God took on human flesh and entered the limits of his created world, in a body, he honoured the created world, and he destroyed sin in the flesh, crucifying it so that we could live these lives in the body to please God, free from sin, led by the Spirit of God, who hovered above the chaos before creation. We become new creations. We can take back our dignity as stewards and caretakers, representing God, ambassadors of the God, who is reconciling all things to himself.

We must take sin seriously. We must take our sin seriously. We do not excuse ourselves from the work and care bestowed upon us to pull up weeds, clean up the water, till the soil, and actively undo the effects of sin. Taking the assignment of creation seriously begins not in anger at the world, but in humility before God the creator, whose creation we are prone to abuse.

• **God will redeem his creation and, the Bible promises, there will be a new heaven and a new earth.** The biblical vision of glory is not us playing harps on clouds in perpetuity, but human beings fully alive in the new heavens and new earth that will be realized when Christ returns. And so our dominion over creation, our work and care, is anticipation. It creates space where that future hope is given witness. We work and care to create plots of *shalom*, even if it is as small as an apartment balcony, the physical body we see (and maybe despise) in the mirror, or the bovine on a grandparent's simple farm.

So what are our tasks in our assignment of creation?

First, to *destroy strongholds*. Our creation assignment includes spiritual battle. Two stronghold extremes exist that impact human interaction with the created world. One is environmentalism as a substitute religion. Here the creature is put in the place of the creator, and humanity is robbed of our God-given dignity and equated with trees and slugs. This becomes its own religion with doomsday, fear-based, truth-twisting, humanity-despising rhetoric. This is a revival of religious animism in our time that has often been deemed "uncivilized." This stronghold is hopeless and leads to fearful submission to powers we were created to rule.

The other extreme is a human-centered domination that can even infect Christians. In the biblical world view, God—not the environment nor humanity—is at the center of all things. When we place ourselves at the center, even as people of faith, we are led to believe and act as if we can do whatever is good for us. But this is our Father's world! Anything else at the center will ultimately slip toward the destruction of the dignity of humanity or the destruction of creation for selfish purposes.

For Christians to dismiss the care of creation because someday the elements will perish in fire (2 Peter 3:10) or God will make a new heaven and a new earth anyway is sadly short-sighted. It is often code for selfishness and a submission to the spiritual powers of comfort, money, and the self. Instead, we must take seriously the gospel of the kingdom revealed in Jesus Christ, in whom God the Father was pleased to fully dwell in this world and through him to reconcile all things to himself, things in heaven and on earth (Colossians 1:19–20).

Our second task in the assignment of creation is to *build up people*.

When we take seriously our assignment of creation, we ultimately build up people, and often the most vulnerable and poor. Studies show that the lack of creation care—polluted waters and smog-laden cities—disproportionately impacts the world's poor. When we respond to the groaning of creation, we are loving God who made it and our neighbours as ourselves.

How can our actions impact the life of children in Delhi, India (which has one of the worst air qualities in the world), or a child living on a First Nations reservation in Canada, where there is no clean water in one of the world's wealthiest countries? God may not assign us to India or place us anywhere near that reservation, but he has assigned us a plot of earth to tread and inhabit each day and given us minds to make decisions on what we purchase, voices to speak, and the will to act toward the well-being and *shalom* of the place where we do live.

Years after Jonah was burped into Nineveh, the kingdom of Assyria fell to Babylon. Babylon was a beast and eventually captured Jonah's people too. The Jews were dragged far from their land and plopped into a foreign puddle. Landless captives, it seemed they had lost all impact and influence. The prophet Jeremiah heard otherwise. He wrote a letter to the exiles in Babylon about how to live their unwelcome assignment.

> "Build houses and settle down; plant gardens and eat what they produce. Marry and have sons and daughters; find wives for your sons and give your daughters in marriage, so that they too may have sons and daughters. Increase in number there; do not decrease. Also, seek the peace and prosperity of the city to which I have carried you into exile. Pray to the LORD for it, because if it prospers, you too will prosper." (Jeremiah 29:5–7)

There it is. You're a captive with a small spot of land that smells and feels different. Among the other routine things of life like starting families, simply plant gardens. In this simple witness of taking seriously the space assigned to you even against your will you are seeking the well-being of even the land of your enemies. You are witnessing to a greater kingdom. You are loving God. You are building up.

My friend Max has a small country property. It has some gardens and a small cottage on the bank of a lazy waterway. Max and Anya love that retreat and take good care of it. In February 2022, Max texted me excitedly. In the grey cold of winter, they had planted some new Thuja trees that will grow and be shelter for birds and hedgehogs. Big deal? It is, when you consider the property is just outside the city limits of Zaporizhzhia, Ukraine, 250 kilometres west of the frontline of what would soon become the greatest European conflict since World War II. With invasion looming—a few weeks later Russian missiles soared over those same trees, unleashing destruction—Max was planting trees. It was a defiant statement of life. It was stewardship, taking back dominion, loving and worshipping God with all that he is and his neighbour as himself in the assignment marked out for him. Max didn't realize, when he celebrated his new trees, that his messing in the dirt would be a story shared to build others up, encouraging people like us to take seriously our own creation assignments. What inspiration might your messing in the dirt provide?

Finally, in our assignments we have a third task: to *live in such a way that we can be entrusted with more.* Isn't someone who commits to life when the world shakes, like Anya and Max, someone worthy of greater entrustment? What little act of care of loving God and living out your dignity as his representative can you practice in your assignment of creation? Do you have a yard, an acreage, a plant in your bedroom, a route you walk that is carelessly littered upon, or a cat or calf to put your arm around? Do you run a business that could make more careful creation care decisions? Have you figured out some "green thumb" ways you can teach others? Do you steward some ancient and indigenous agrarian practices that should be passed on? Do decisions on how money is invested rest with you? If we told stories about what you do with the assignment of creation, would you be entrusted with more?

You have a creation assignment given by Sovereign God. What will you do with it to love him with all you are and your neighbour as yourself?

## QUESTIONS FOR THIS ASSIGNMENT

• What parts of creation have been entrusted to you to steward?

• How does God use the natural world to bless you?

• How might your fellowship of Christians be more purposeful in the care of creation?

• How is the Spirit inviting you to take steps to act against the destruction of God's world?

# CHAPTER 5
# YOUR HOUSEHOLD IS YOUR ASSIGNMENT

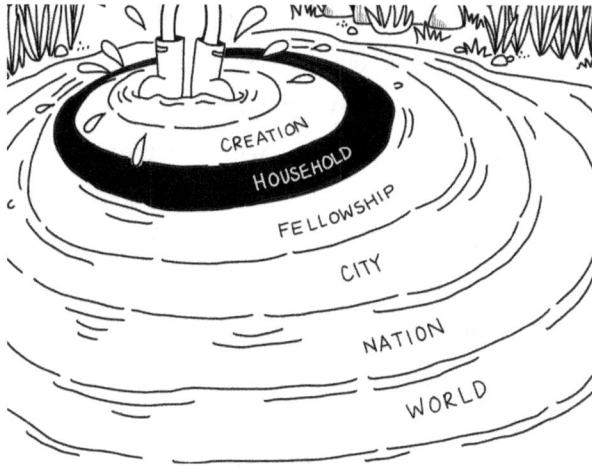

S overeign God has given us life assignments.

In every assignment, God sets us apart to represent him. We are ambassadors of Christ. "Let your kingdom come, your will be done on earth as it is in heaven" is our prayer, and we are enlisted by God to part of the answer to it.

We come to our next assignment: your household.

A church I served as pastor was confronted with an enormous challenge when the husband in a significant family was discovered having an affair. The guy had come from a difficult background and had given his life to Christ when he was dating his wife. He had grown as a disciple over the years in leaps and bounds. Before the marriage, the woman's parents were of course uncomfortable with her dating a non-Christian, but they had patiently embraced him, and when he became a Christian, they were overjoyed. They became the family he never had.

As a result of all this love and transformation, the gut-wrenching news of infidelity rocked everyone. People rallied to love the woman, the wider family, and even the man we were all really, really perturbed with. I remember sitting with the woman's parents, who were pig farmers and highly respected elders in the church. They radiated the love of Christ. They listened well and asked great questions, were deep theologically and rich in wisdom, and when they spoke, everyone listened. But now they were broken. They wept and said something profound: "From the time our kids were little we prayed for the spouses they would marry. So we prayed for this man, which means that God knew this. Which means we will walk through it with him." I suddenly knew why they were so respected. They knew how to live the assignment of this household in a Christ-centered way as 1 Timothy 3:5 says: "If anyone does not know how to manage his own [household],[4] how can he take care of God's church?"

It took a long time, but their son-in-law who made such a big mistake, repented, and surrendered himself entirely into God's hands. He gave to God what is God's and became a model of grace, humility, and joy. A boisterous community party celebrated the renewal of the couple's vows. And then, a year later this man who had almost destroyed his home—my friend who taught me so much about confession and humility—died of cancer. But because of the strength of the Christ-centered, Christlike household who enveloped him even his mournful funeral was a celebration too.

You have a household assignment.

The word *family* can be a loaded and layered term. Does a family consist of parents (or parent) with children? Does it refer to the circle including aunts, uncles, cousins, and grandparents? Is it a tribal identity, as in some cultures? What family means may depend on where you're from or who you're from. In a sign that there is great longing for familial ties, the term is now applied to the culture a business tries to create for its employees or a team sets for its players. "They are like family to me" can be interpreted both positively, as in "they loved

---

[4] The Greek word here is *oikou*, which is used throughout the New Testament to refer to all the inhabitants of one's household, not only one's closest biological "family" as often understood in contemporary western contexts. It is also the term used to refer to the household or family of God in 1 Timothy 3:15.

and embraced me like my home did"—or negatively, as in "they were better to me than my home was."

A television advertisement finds a teenage boy coming home from school, listening to a message from his mom saying she can't be home, and he'll have to eat alone and get himself to his sports event. He does so despairingly and then waits for a ride. When it arrives, he is welcomed into a vehicle with his teammates. He's suddenly smilingly "at home." The implied message is that when your family lets you down—as all our families do in some way—those who drive this vehicle won't. The family images in the commercial are telling: "Family" is on the one hand reduced to a son who eats alone and a mom who is doing her gosh-darn best. On the other hand, family is seen as something longed for and more fully found outside your immediate relations. Since the 1960s Western society has diminished family to the smallest common denominator— at best a mom and dad, two kids, and a pet, or even what the boy experiences in the commercial. Western society, with its drive toward individualism and self-determination, chipped away perhaps irreparably at the first foundation every human being was intended to start life from. Does anyone really know what "family values" means anymore?

Family is where, as Lesslie Newbigin wrote in *Foolishness to the Greeks*, "one is not free to choose his company and where one is not free to pursue self-interest to the limit."[5] In other words, family— central in God's foundational plan for being human—puts boundaries on life from the very beginning. From our first breath we are limited to a start we did not choose, with people we did not choose, where we are not free to only do as we wish or only be with whom we wish. Even a baby abandoned at birth, or a toddler adopted outside their birth family is immediately limited by forces beyond their control that will irreversibly impact their life's trajectory. We are always in some way limited by where life begins. Consequently, and inevitably, family is always one of our God-given assignments.

---

[5] Lesslie Newbigin, *Foolishness to the Greeks* (Grand Rapids: Eerdmans, 1986), 113.

This is why, when my family was separated by four thousand kilometres from my mom when she was in a nursing home, I called her every day. There are many people in nursing homes, but I called that wheelchair-bound woman in that small town in that small room her life was now reduced to. This is why migrant workers seek jobs in Europe to make it possible for their entire household to live better back "home." Billions of dollars criss-cross the globe for this reason every year. This is why when we're teenagers our parents might frustrate or embarrass us, but when we hold our own child, we turn to those we thought didn't know what they were doing to learn what to do. This is why when the home disintegrates, we not only suffer individually or as a small, related unit but tear the wider social fabric we are part of.

When society undermines the household as an assignment worthy of the highest dignity, it is cannibalizing and destroying itself. That car advertisement reveals the pitiful end of Western individualism and the concept of family: a boy eating alone and the cry from a generation longing for a place to call home even if just for a few minutes in the back of someone else's vehicle.

We all have a God-given household assignment that is not anyone else's responsibility.

The Bible is a family book. In fact, it's a family story—the story of the family of God. Scripture begins with creation, with the first family, and tells multiple genealogical stories. The Old Testament book of 1 Chronicles begins with nine entire chapters of genealogy. The arrival of Jesus in both Matthew and Luke is rooted in the long family story of God's work in history. God's acting to save humanity from disintegration under the rule of sin and death is aimed at creating a family for himself.

Family is rooted in the very nature of God, who is family himself—Father, Son, and Spirit. The Spirit hovered over the chaos of the disordered expanse. In creating us, God said, "Let *us* make humankind in *our* image, in *our* likeness, so that *they* may rule" (Genesis 1:26, italics added). Our corporate work and care of God's creation is rooted in us being the representation of God's diverse oneness. The image of God is not male or female individuals, but male *and* female in union ("in the image of God he created them; male and female he created them"; Genesis 1:27). Humanity is blessed to multiply offspring, produce family after family, who will be God's representatives in the world. The image of God is, therefore, visible in the community of family, of belonging, of mutuality, of working together—not alone—in the assignment given.

Jesus was born into a family within the limits of a particular time, place, and even reputation (one of his own disciples wasn't sure anything good could come from Nazareth). Jesus took the limits of his own family seriously. On the cross, he asked one of his disciples to look after his mom. Yet Jesus routinely called God his Father. He lived in an intimate relationship with his heavenly *Abba*. As an adolescent, he told Mary and Joseph that he must be in his Father's house, the temple in Jerusalem, and at the same time lived obediently with them (Luke 2:49–52). He wanted desperately to please his Dad in heaven (John 4:34; Luke 22:42). He taught his disciples to make his Father their Father and to pray to our Father in heaven. He lived a holy tension between two households. We see this pronounced at the wedding in Cana when Jesus accepts—though with some initial hesitancy—his mom's bold push from the shadows into the unveiling of his divine identity by turning water to wine (John 2:3–5). It is not insignificant that God the Son and the Son of Man step into view as one at a wedding—the joyful celebration of a new household.

Not unlike us, family wasn't always easy for Jesus. When his family observed his popularity and tried to talk some sense into him, he seemed almost dismissive. Instead, he expanded the notion of what family is in God's sight: "'Who is my mother, and who are my brothers?' And stretching out his hand toward his disciples, he said, 'Here are my mother and my brothers! For whoever does the will of my Father in heaven is my brother and sister and mother'" (Matthew

12:48–50 ESV). God's family are those do the will of their heavenly Father and represent him in the world.

When describing the church God is forming from every language, nation, and language, Paul wrote, "Through him we both have access to the Father by one Spirit. Consequently, you are no longer foreigners and strangers, but fellow citizens with God's people and also members of his household" (Ephesians 2:18–19). Every local expression of Christians reflects the family of God—a people we didn't choose, but with whom we come to do life by God's choosing and grace. In the local church, we are seeking to do the will of our Father in heaven together. The rich diversity of the body of Christ is a household that reflects God himself; that is his image. And so, when Paul described who should lead these local households of God with all their warts and differences, he said, "If anyone does not know how to manage his own [household], how can he take care of God's church?" (1 Timothy 3:5).

And so, it comes full circle.

We are made in God's image, and God is a communion of one (Father, Son, and Spirit). There are not three gods, but one God expressed in the mysterious unity of three persons; just as I am one man but also a son, husband, and father.

God's plan for creation is entrusted and bound to the families of the earth who are made in his image and hinges on whether they will walk in humility and relationship with him or not.

But we sought our own way. We ran like prodigals from our true home, and sin and its dire consequences wrecked us.

God's plan to save his creation from the grip of sin and death came as God the Son humbled himself to the limits of a family unit (Mary and Joseph) and the larger family story of the Jewish people.

God's rescues and reconciles us through Jesus's cross, resurrection, and ascension. In God the Son, every barrier that separates us from our Father *and* one another crumbles. Jesus is our conquering big brother, who reconciles us to our heavenly Father. The Father adopts us into his household, giving us full rights and privileges as children of God. The Holy Spirit, through whom we cry *Abba*, fills us and guarantees our unchallenged position as heirs in the household of God.

The way we discern who leads the local expression of this great household of faith is to look to those who care for and manage their own households well. The fellowship looks for those who look like their Father in heaven. Which is why the couple in the church I served were absolutely the right kind of disciples to lead a local church because their household, while far from perfect and not without its grief and pain, was its own household of God.

And that's why our household is a crucial assignment given by Sovereign God, with all its limits, challenges and tests. In our households, it is quickly revealed whether we have come under the authority of God the Father or not.

Paul exhorted Christians to put off the old self with its practices (like anger, slander, sexual immorality, greed, and lying) and put on the new self that is being renewed in knowledge after the image of its Creator (Colossians 3:5–11). In doing so, he used language that referred to the household of God (vs. 12ff.). The household of God is to reflect the household culture set by our heavenly Father. And these new qualities—just like the ways of the old self—are always lived out with others, particularly in our households.

The image of God in us that was restored through Jesus is to be seen in how wives submit to their husbands, how husbands love their wives, how children honour their parents, how parents shape the next generation, how slaves relate to their masters, and how masters relate to their slaves (Colossians 3:18–4:1). The household assignment is for everyone in every age group, married or single (both states are dignified and beautiful in God's eyes). And the household (Greek word *oikos*) is broader than the nuclear family. The household Paul described as the crucible of the new self encompasses those for whom we have special responsibility and those with whom we live in closest proximity and partnership.

The language of slaves and masters is unsettling, but a Roman slave—someone bound to serve in a household—was as much a part of the family as anyone else. The ancient households Paul knew were not mom, dad, two kids, and a lizard, but the sphere of nearest and dearest relationships a person had unique responsibility for. The responsibility of living the renewed image of God was shared by all parties. The Christian household will increasingly steward and become like God together to be a familial representation of God the Father in the world. Hence, the key locale for Christianity's undoing of slavery in the Roman Empire were these households that lived counterculturally (read Paul's letter to Philemon).

Women. Men. Wives. Husbands. Boys. Girls. Singles. Partnered. Those uniquely bound to our household (like that unfaithful son-in-law, or like my "brother" Larry, who was not my blood relation but came into my home when I was ten, or the students my family has welcomed over the years, or the employee that has a unique relationship with your family, or the roommates you suddenly find yourself cooking with)—these are our unique household assignment. No one else on the planet has the same kind of responsibility for them that we do.

Are we beginning to see that our household assignment is bigger than first assumed?

Let's get practical.

What household capital do you have? What has Sovereign God entrusted your home with, and how are you investing it to build a household that represents God in the world? Mike Breen and Ben Sternke describe five capitals or areas of investment for the Christ-centered household[6] (in ascending order):

---

[6] Mike Breen and Ben Sternke, *Oikonomics: How to Invest in Life's Five Capitals the Way Jesus Did* (Pawleys Island: 3 Dimension Ministries, 2014), 40.

- **Financial capital: how much treasure (dollars and cents) we must invest.** This grows or diminishes over time, often by forces out of our control, but no matter the amount or if we think we have enough, our household must steward finances.

- **Intellectual capital: how much creativity, ideas, and knowledge we must invest.** Money is less valuable than our household's minds, ingenuity, and what inspires and moves us.

- **Physical capital: how much time and energy we must invest.** How do we expend the limits of our household time, health, and strength? Each day, we steward physical capital we cannot get back.

- **Relational capital: how much relational equity we must invest.** This is the quality and quantity of our household and friend relationships. This is limited because we can handle only so many of these, and with everyone we love, we only have limited years.

- **Spiritual capital: the depth of our relationship with God and the spiritual equity we must invest.** The wisdom, power, authority, truth, and freedom God alone gives constitute true wealth and abundance.

All these household capitals come from God and are entrusted to us. In the assignment of our household, we are stewarding each capital and constantly investing. How we invest them will shape those we have responsibility for and the society our household is part of.

In what order does our household place these capitals? What do our actions reveal about what is of greatest priority? Are they all embraced as our household's responsibility? What would our children say has priority? How we form our households often depends on our experience in the households we grew up in. If our home placed high value on intellectual capital, we may have secured a top-flight education and a fantastic career, but they may have come at the expense of spiritual capital. Or if our home valued physical capital, then we may have thrived athletically while everything else—from financial capital to relational capital—centered around that sport. And what happens when the sport is done?

God desires for our households to thrive in all five capitals because he has sovereignly given them to us, with unique strengths to steward. Jesus told the Samaritan woman at the local well that the life he gives is a deep well of living water overflowing into eternal life (John 4:14). The life Jesus gives waters everything else. We must invest as though the most important things *are* the most important.

Since we are created in the image of God, spiritual capital should receive highest value—not at the expense of the others, but to ground them. The lower value capitals are made beautiful and transformational by the more valuable. The lower should always serve the greater. Furthermore, every capital is best lived when we take time to grow them, when we don't chase quick fixes but invest for the long haul. The household challenge is setting the right order. The household privilege is stewarding them to the glory of God. After all, how we invest in those we have unique responsibility for will water ourselves, those we have been given to love and mature, and the society we inhabit and help form.

Many household questions suddenly emerge if we are to destroy strongholds, build up people, and live in such a way that we can be entrusted with more.

**Where does our financial capital go?** Are we modeling financial wisdom and cheerful generosity? Do we serve money or steward it? Do we try to keep up with or love our neighbours? Are we envious, complaining, or thankful? Do we value people based on their economic status? Are we earning to bring more of the world's wealth under the stewardship of ambassadors of Christ or simply earning to build our own empires?

**How do we spend intellectual capital?** Do we strengthen our minds and learn how to think well? Do we read widely and wisely? Do we have lively, even disagreeing conversation? Do we embrace the gift of boredom that stimulates creativity? Do we wrestle with new, and old, ideas? Do we know the history that has shaped us and that we are building upon? Do we engage the news of the world? Do we try new things in God's great big world?

**What about physical capital?** How are we stewarding our bodies? Are we couch potatoes? Do we seek recreation at the expense of the other capitals? Do we value sweating and labouring together for the common good? How do we practice rest and value sabbath?

**What relationships do we invest in?** Are they only for self-interest? Are we befriending people other than those we like, who are like us and fit our economic bracket, ethnicity, or culture? Do we love being with people Jesus loves but who don't yet love him? Do we practice hospitality? Do we value learning how to maintain reconciled relationships? Do we practice listening, forgiveness, perseverance, patience, grace, and mercy as we stumble our way toward maturity? Do our households produce reconcilers in workplaces, schools, and the households they will one day have responsibility for? Is our home a respite and refuge for the orphan and widow, for the neglected, ignored, and vulnerable?

**How do we invest our spiritual capital, the deep well that waters everything else?** Are we valuing spiritual community and the wonder of Jesus's church? Do we have spiritual conversations? Do we discern our finances, intellectual pursuits, physical bodies, and relationships through the lens of what pleases our heavenly Father? Does Scripture shape us? Are we praying together, and for what? How do we interpret and face suffering and trials? Do younger generations hear the stories of God's faithfulness from the older? Are children's straightforwardness and youthful zeal (and occasional irreverence) welcome? Do we teach spiritual discernment? Do we know how to interpret the times and the shifts and drifts of culture without fear and while remaining faithful to Jesus Christ as Lord?

Whether married or single, with kids or childless; whether home is with the family we were born into or with those who were once strangers but have welcomed us in, we all have primary household relationships that are our assignment. Children too share this household assignment. As children we belong to a "home" we didn't choose. God gave it to us. We share the household assignment with the "big" people we are to honour. Today's children will steward future households that will carry forward the representation of God in the world.

So, kids: you're not just living at home till you launch. You are already participating in household-building! Your role may look different than an adult's, but since God put you where he did, you need to be involved in the assignment God gives your household. Children are not household passengers—they are full-fledged participants. Every day for every age is household-building practice. The everyday life of everyone in a Christ-centered household—playing; working in the kitchen, garage, or garden; learning Bach; riffing guitar; praying, resolving conflicts, snuggling, or engaging neighbours; discerning the use of technology; discussing the news, a book, or a movie, and even shopping – is the work of ambassadors who are "assuming together their responsibility for the whole world."[7] The adults in the room must delight in innocent faith and determinedly include children in this grand responsibility, just as Jesus did. The children in the room must receive, not reject, the household God has given and increase in wisdom, stature, and favour with God and others, just as Jesus did. The household assignment requires a multigenerational and intergenerational investment.

These vital household capitals we share responsibility for must be submitted to Christ. If not, they become strongholds in need of

---

[7] Johannes Reimer. *Family in Mission: Theology and Praxis* (Carlisle: Langham, 2020), 25.

demolition. The financial, intellectual, physical, and relational can become enslaving powers. Even spirituality can be a destructive stronghold if we have built our spiritual source in that which is not rooted in God but in ideologies, philosophies, or spiritual forces and practices that are not centered in Jesus Christ, who came to set us free.

Furthermore, these capitals are ultimately invested to build up people we love! This is one of life's great tasks, for the household is the first place we are formed and sent from into God's big world. Our household assignment is not the retirement we are securing or a nice house, but the people we build up to be ambassadors of God's reconciling kingdom.

We should live, even in our household, in such a way that we can be invested with more. Parents, grandparents, and aunts and uncles know which children in the clan can be entrusted with more. Being given more isn't really about age or personality; it is about the fruit we bear, our character, and our trustworthiness. A lack of these holy qualities at home will show up elsewhere and can erode our influence and our society. Who we are at home paves the way for what comes when we leave home. And managing our household well, as Paul says in 1 Timothy 3, will influence our next assignment, the fellowship, and every other assignment God gives those who launch from the place called home.

## QUESTIONS FOR THIS ASSIGNMENT

- Who do you have unique household responsibility for now?

- What strongholds exist within your household that need to be addressed?

- Who do you know that lives this assignment well and that you could learn from?

- What experiences or aspirations does your household have that are clues to the unique way God wants to use you in the world?

# CHAPTER 6
# YOUR FELLOWSHIP IS YOUR ASSIGNMENT

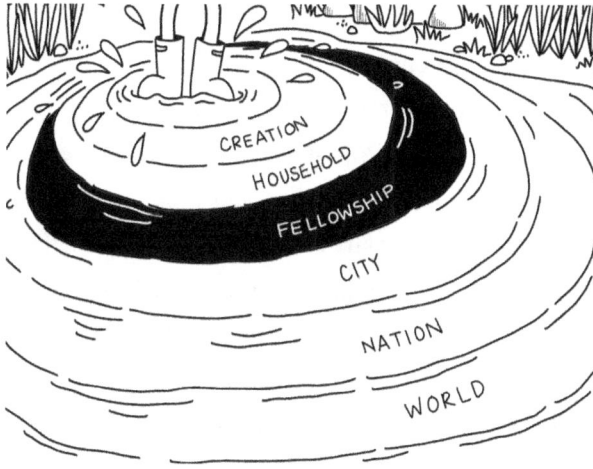

In the puddle of life, we discover God has given gifts, personalities, and limitations that we are to receive and surrender to our maker in order that his glory might fill the universe. We are ambassadors and representatives of Christ, and he commissions us into this holy project.

We turn now to the assignment of the fellowship.

To be Christian is to be church. Church is not a place you go, or a non-profit you volunteer with. The church is a glorious wonder and miracle: God's reconciled people who follow Jesus as Lord and are the community through whom the endless wisdom of God is being made known from the most visible street corner to the invisible, but no less real, rulers and authorities in the heavenly realms (Ephesians 3:10). To be Christian is to be church that is eternal, historical, global, and local. Our local church—no matter its size or tradition or whether it is three hundred years old or a three-week old plant—is just one organ, blood vessel, or molecule in Jesus's body.

Our local church is a fellowship. The Greek word translated "fellowship" in the English New Testament is *koinonia*, which means partnership or shared participation. Our local fellowship is the experience and expression of the household of God where we live. Our local fellowship is the proclamation and demonstration of the gospel of God's rule and kingdom where we call home. Our local fellowship takes responsibility for one another, for the unity of Christians, and for the well-being of the geography we call home. The fellowship is not one person or position (like a pastor or elder) but the people, a shared partnership or participation of sisters and brothers beneath the good gaze of our heavenly Father and under our head pastor-shepherd, Jesus Christ, the Lord of the church. It is *we*, the fellowship, who have a shared assignment to follow Jesus in unity, learning to walk out together God's character and be his representation in the world. Our local fellowship is the body of Christ.

9.79*

Does that number ring a bell? I remember being glued to the television as a sixteen-year-old watching the 100-meter men's final at the 1988 Summer Olympic Games in Seoul, South Korea. The long-anticipated battle between America's Carl Lewis and Canada's Ben Johnson was about to be waged. As a Canadian, I saw it as the brash big brother versus the underdog immigrant. National pride was on the line. And then in 9.79 seconds it was over! Ben Johnson blew by his competitors, obliterated the world record, and raised his arm in celebration a full length ahead of a stunned Carl Lewis. I was beyond thrilled.

The next day everything fell apart. A shameful disbelief overcame my country when it was announced that Johnson's mandatory urine sample revealed traces of steroids. Johnson cheated. My youthful heart broke. It crushed Canadian national identity and challenged our altruistic self-image.

Anyone observing Ben Johnson's body critically over the years leading up to Seoul could have noticed something wasn't normal. His bulging muscles and unexpected rise to prominence should have raised flags. Of course, he wasn't the only athlete looking like that or doing what he was doing in those days, so we happily doubted the puffed-up realities of our heroes for the sake of ten seconds of glory. But when it all came crashing down, it suddenly mattered very much how the body was built. The test, of course, only exposed reality: a body that was not stewarded with care but manipulated by Johnson's trainers and handlers. For a fleeting moment the toast of the Olympic Games, Johnson was banned for life from international track and field competition. His blazing 9.79 world record received a telling asterisk (it took another eleven years for another man to be clocked travelling 100 meters that quickly). In the years that followed, Johnson became a sad and almost comedic figure as he sought to redeem his reputation, even racing horses a decade after the glory and disgrace of Seoul as a festival sideshow.

What does Ben Johnson's 9.79* have to do with our assignment in the fellowship?

"Now you are the body of Christ, and each one of you is a part of it" (1 Corinthians 12:27). This is what Paul said to the very troubled local fellowship of disciples in the ancient Greek city of Corinth. They were imperfect. They were messy and frustrating to Paul, who loved them and sought to mature them into their assignment. Yet as confounding as they were, as manipulated by outside voices and prone to bloated dysfunction as they were, they were still the body of Christ.

When Jesus walked out of the tomb and appeared to the disciples, he invited Thomas, who was struggling to come to grips with the possibility of resurrection, to touch the scars caused by the brutality of first-century Roman crucifixion (John 20:26–27). Jesus's resurrected body did not have scars removed or airbrushed away; instead they were redeemed and exchanged. His scars went from marks of defeat to marks of victory. The scars themselves were reconciled, just as they were the vehicle of our reconciliation to God and one another. Jesus's resurrected body was not the "perfect" body magazines and advertisements tempt us to pursue. Jesus's body was fully authentic and carried a new, unstoppable authority. His body, the church, expressed in local fellowships in every little corner of the world, is this too: the bearers of earthly authenticity and divine authority.

Jesus's body is his *ekklesia*. This is the Greek word translated "church" in English Bibles, used by Jesus when he said, "I will build my church, and the gates of Hades will not overcome it" (Matthew 16:18). Hades was the ancient Greek description of the unseen, freaky place where all the dead and departed resided. *Ekklesia* was originally used for those who sit at the city gates, a town council, who make decisions for the direction and way of life of a place. Used as it is in Matthew 16, the *ekklesia* is in direct contrast to the gates of darkness and death. There is a conflict of visions for the common good—one shaped by a living community under the Lordship of Jesus as Messiah and Son of God and the other designed by strongholds of the dead and hell that offer nothing to the living and seek to steal, kill, and destroy life in all its God-intended fullness. The gates of Hades do not care about God's best for people or creation; they are governors of the grave and self-interest. The *ekklesia* is about life and vibrant flourishing in the world God created. Hades is about death, escape, and the zombie apocalypse.

In naming his body the *ekklesia*, Jesus indicates we are those, as Johannes Reimer writes in *Missio Politica*, "called out of the world to become light for the world, accepting responsibility for the world and transforming the world into a place according to the teaching of Jesus on the kingdom of God."[8] The *ekklesia* is, as Dietrich Bonhoeffer wrote in a letter from a Nazi prison during World War II, "not conceiving ourselves religiously as specially favoured, but as wholly belonging to the world. Then Christ is no longer an object of religion, but something quite different, indeed and in truth the Lord of the world."[9]

---

[8] Johannes Reimer, *Missio Politica: The Mission of the Church and Politics* (Carlisle: Langham, 2017), 48.

[9] Dietrich Bonhoeffer, *Letters and Papers from Prison* (London: Collins, 1963), 92.

The body of Christ is meant to be this *ekklesia* of authenticity and authority. A "church" is not a building but a local fellowship of unlikely people who belong authentically to their world to make Jesus's authority visible as the light of the world. Sovereign God has given every disciple of every gender and age an assignment to make Jesus's body healthy. Each Christian has a role in helping the body run with integrity, authenticity, and authority as ambassadors of the kingdom of heaven in very normal, beautiful, and messy places like Corinth and the crossroads, towns, and cities we call home.

Jesus said that upon the confession that he is the Messiah, the Son of the Living God, he will build his church and that the gates of Hades will not overcome it. This authentic, confessing community will have authority to unlock heaven in the world they live in (Matthew 16:13–20). Jesus cast this grand vision in the region of Jerusalem at a time when Jews were waiting for a king to make Israel great again. He declared it under the domination of Rome, which ruled as an oppressing, colonizing empire. He spoke it over a small fellowship of simple people with no power or privilege—fishers and tax collectors, former prostitutes, and outlawed political zealots. Jesus said that it would be the love shared within this fellowship that would show the world who he is and what God's reign looks like when all is falling apart (John 13:35). And Jesus said that when he left and the Holy Spirit had come upon his followers, this partnership of unlikely undesirables would do greater things than he had done (John 14:12), becoming his witnesses in Jerusalem and Judea and Samaria and to the ends of the earth (Acts 1:8).

From the very beginning of his ministry Jesus had been describing—and modelling—the qualities and nature of the *ekklesia* fellowship he was forming.

Jesus called us salt and light (Matthew 5:13–16). Salt has long-lasting preserving power and makes things really yummy. Un-salty salt does nothing for your dinner and isn't even good for melting ice on a sidewalk. Light in a city or a house—as the first hearers would have heard it—was not a switch to flip, but something to be tended. A person looking for hope-giving light in the fearful darkness of the countryside depended upon those carefully tended household lights in that city up on the hill. In the ancient world, salt and light were not quick processes, nor were they options. They were necessities to be stewarded for life to thrive. Salt and light are what Jesus said we are. This is an identity we tend as the fellowship of his people. And this saltiness and light are for the good of the earth; to be tasted and seen so that the salty and light-giving life of Jesus's disciples causes people to give glory to God the Father. The fellowship exists so that the reign of God is tasted and seen! "Taste and see that the LORD is good" (Psalm 34:8).

Now what is this the salt and light fellowship like?

Jesus's Sermon on the Mount begins with what have been called the Beatitudes (from the Latin word *beati*, meaning happy, contented, or blessed) in Matthew 5:3–12. They describe the enviable life—the life that is blessed, the life we've always wanted, the life that flourishes. They are the qualities of salt and light. They are also counter-intuitive to what we are tempted to believe life is all about. They are also impossible to live without fellowship—without partnership with others. Each one is plural: "those, theirs, they, they, theirs." Each is a way of life in a world that puffs you up or crushes you:

- Poverty of spirit—humility that recognizes the desperate need for God rather than pride in self-reliance or self-determination;

- Mourning—grieving with God over the state of the world; within us, among us, and beyond us;

- Meekness—surrendering to God's power and leading. It is yoking to Jesus (Matthew 11:29). The Greek word *praus* referred to the harnessing of a horse, or power under control;

86

- Hungering and thirsting for righteousness—craving the right way of living and what is right in society because we know and desire God's character and will;

- Mercifulness—giving to others what is undeserved because we have not received what we ourselves deserved;

- Purity of heart—a cleansing of motives that enables us to engage the world as God does;

- Peacemaking—the work of reconciling and ending strife is the mark of God's children; and

- Being persecuted for righteousness' sake—mistreated because too much of the character of Jesus is evident; reviled because the right living we hunger for is spilling over into our prophetic way of life in society. This is the very stuff that got Jesus in trouble with the powers that be.

These beautiful beatitudes are Jesus's first words in Matthew about the fellowship of the king. These are the qualities of the salt and light fellowship. This ought to be how we measure the quality of the fellowship we are becoming locally. Tending to the health of this in the body is our assignment, or else we lose our saltiness, the city on the hill will go dark, and no one will be able to find the way home!

How do we maintain this salt and light, this blessed and enviable way in the local fellowship?

First, *we demolish strongholds*. We fight a spiritual battle. We wage war against powers of darkness. We confront prayerfully and with Scripture lofty arguments that are set up against the ways of God. We do this with and for the fellowship so that we are not a puffed up, unhealthy body risking disqualification. It is sobering that Jesus bluntly called out what is unhealthy, even threatening to shut down five of seven local church fellowships addressed in Revelation 2–3. Jesus wants us to battle for a healthy fellowship.

Taking down the strongholds that can diminish saltiness and light requires maintaining the confession upon which Jesus said he will build his church: that Jesus is the Messiah, the Christ, the Son of the living God (Matthew 16:16). This is what Hades, darkness, and the demons can't stand against. We confess the identity of him who is the light of the world (John 8:12). We embody this confession in the blessed life of the Beatitudes. "Jesus is Lord" is the confession for which Christians deem it worthy to joyfully face persecution. This requires our ongoing repentance; our contending for the unity of the Spirit and the bond of peace (Ephesians 4:3–6).

When our devoted fellowship shares a vibrant commitment to the apostles' teaching, breaking bread, and prayer (Acts 2:42), we are regularly renewing this confession. This renewal of the confession with others where we live demolishes strongholds that quickly arise—like the weeds we pluck up only to have them spring back or like the dust we wipe only to have it settle again. This confession is personal and communal. This confessional work, this realignment requires perseverance and relationship. The fellowship's work in worship, studying Scripture, communion, prayer, generosity, service, and application is not to create a personal spiritual experience but to demolish the strongholds we have set up or accepted. When we gather as a fellowship, when we "go to church," we are not going to consume information: we're in fellowship to wage war! We gather to name Jesus Lord, get back on our knees, and expose and name whatever has become strongholds needing demolition—like the idea that cultural agendas guide the fellowship, that political power is what the *ekklesia* should grasp, or that consumerist cravings are what the church is here to serve.

This requires a commitment to partner in discerning and obeying what Jesus is saying now as we live in the moment we have been given. The New Testament pleads for Christians not to give up meeting together. In being with each other, we hold fast to the confession that

Jesus is Lord and has overcome, and we spur one another on toward love and good deeds (Hebrews 10:19–25). If we give up being in fellowship, the result is not that we will cease to have a confession but that we will replace the confession we are to steward for this generation with something else. If we don't kneel before King Jesus, we will kneel before a stronghold that is not worthy of those made in the image of God. Christians in every age and historical context are tempted to confess the lofty opinions of their day, which are governed by Hades. If we surrender to the strongholds rather than demolishing them, we will become unsalty, and the light will go out. We will become a puffed-up body and eventually a pitiful facsimile of the glory we were to have.

We also maintain our salt and light by *building up people*. In Romans 12:1–2, Paul called Christians to marvel at God's merciful plan to bring orphans like us into his family. In Jesus Christ, God has rescued us from the eternally fatal effects of sin, the internal lack of peace we all carry, and the judgements we make of others. He has made us his very own Spirit-filled children. God's mysterious plan to bring all people, Jew and Gentile, female and male, young and old, together into his family should cause us to offer our bodies with all their limits as living sacrifices. We die to ourselves, give ourselves into God's hands, seek to understand his will, and live his ways as ambassadors of heaven. The community where this new surrendered life is learned and lived is the local fellowship of the saints.

To use a metaphor, our fellowship is the practice field of becoming God's team. Our practice regimen is described in Romans 12:3–21 (perhaps pause to read this passage now). The task in our assignment is to offer the limits and extent of who we are and what we have been given to build up our local fellowship. We have different gifts from the Spirit that we are to exercise. No one gift is best or most important. The gifts we have been given are for—as Paul said in 1 Corinthians 12—the common good.

Our assignment is to build up the fellowship, the people, and capacity of our local *ekklesia*. This is the whole task of the whole people of God. Because we have given ourselves first to God, we now offer ourselves—our gifts, resources, personal spirituality, maturing, and salt and light obedience (Romans 12:9–21)—to the fellowship. However, if we offer our gifts and resources to build up the fellowship while we tear it down with an unwillingness to love one another, we are just producing irritating noise (1 Corinthians 13:1). Doing our part while not associating with those who are poor or considered lowly (James 2:1–7) or living at war with another believer that we are unwilling to reconcile with (Matthew 5:23–24) is empty hypocrisy and a denial of the gospel. Our God-given gifts, our Spirit-formed character, and our willingness to practice being salt and light in the fellowship are what builds up the fellowship. This takes time and tending. So no matter our age, ethnicity, or history, if we have offered ourselves to God as a living sacrifice, we have chores in his household.

You have an assignment within the limits of the fellowship where God has placed you.

God assigns our fellowships. Some of us are born into a fellowship. This should never be quickly dismissed or taken for granted. Some of us come into a fellowship because the people who introduced us to Jesus brought us in. This should be received as if being born into a family we will grow in and help thrive. Some of us must choose a fellowship because we moved to a new community or country. This we should discern prayerfully and carefully based on how our gifts, needs, and mission and the fellowship's gifts, needs, and mission converge into what will bring mutual blessing and multiplying blessing.

We should receive the fellowship as God's choosing, not the equivalent of picking the restaurant we like or the movie we want to see (even if some fellowships meet in theatres). It is not uncommon for contemporary Christians, formed by the strongholds of consumerism and the tyranny of the self, to choose "their church" based on music, programming, or a celebrity pastor. Conversely, Christians leave fellowships because of personal offense (as if we've never offended others!) or personal dissatisfaction (as if the purpose of the fellowship is to satisfy or entertain us!). Our fellowships exist to become a city on a hill, a communion of salt and light, a healthy body, receiving one another—including other fellowships that comprise the *ekklesia* in our towns and cities—as a gift of Sovereign God for our maturity and for his ministry of reconciliation in a broken world. We all have a role to play in building up God's household of faith!

The first disciples did not choose each other. Jesus chose them on purpose and with purpose. They struggled to build each other up, but that was precisely the task Jesus called them to. The first disciples argued and were disgruntled with each other (Mark 10:35–45). Are we so different?

To be Christian is to receive the limits of the fellowship Jesus chose for us. When we receive the assignment of building up a healthy body, we will experience the joy of offering our gifts, character, and spiritual growth as Romans 12 describes. We will experience the joy of receiving from others. We will joyfully share from our financial, intellectual, physical, and relational capital because we are privileged to build up the fellowship that is salt and light, *ekklesia*, where we live. Our task is not to create successful religious organizations, but to build up a healthy body our Father can be proud of (John 5:44). We exercise because, to adapt the words of Scottish Olympian Eric Liddell in the film *Chariots of Fire*, "We believe that God made us for a purpose. But he also made us fast, and when we run, we feel his pleasure."

God's glory will fill the universe, and his mysterious and messy church—local and global—is central in that plan. Your assignment is to build up the fellowship of the saints Jesus has chosen for you. When we offer our Spirit-given gifts, our Spirit-formed character, and our Christ-centered salt and light obedience to build up, we become known and tested. We will mature and thrive and be about our third task in our assignments: living in such a way that we can be entrusted with more. Live in the assignment of your fellowship in such a way that the fellowship might entrust you with more blessing, more influence, and expanded borders. Be known. Be a servant. Be a builder. Be the qualities of Romans 12. Be a healthy organ for a healthy body. After all, your city is watching. And your world is searching for a city on a hill.

## QUESTIONS FOR THIS ASSIGNMENT

- How would you describe your fellowship, and what do you love most about it?

- What unique gifts and strengths does your fellowship have to share with the world?

- What contribution do you have to make to the health and vitality of your fellowship? What do others notice about you and invite you to contribute? If no one notices you, what might you need to change?

- What have you experienced to be the greatest blessings and challenges of living in fellowship?

# CHAPTER 7

## YOUR CITY IS YOUR ASSIGNMENT

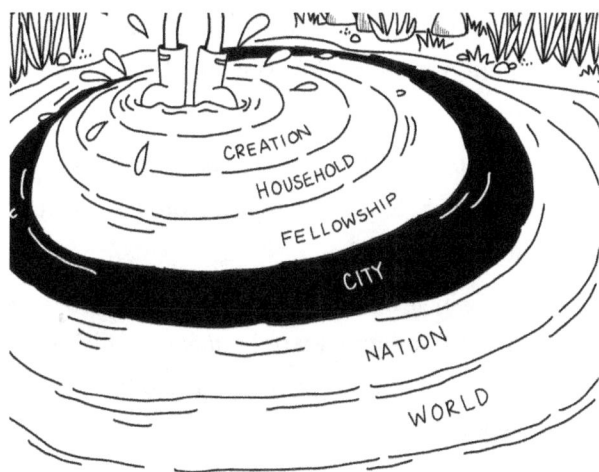

Christians are the ambassadors of Christ, ministers of reconciliation; fragile jars carrying what we are learning is God's very best, his shalom, into every assignment he has for us as he fills the universe with his glory.

We just finished considering the assignment of the Christian fellowship, but a fellowship does not exist on a cloud or in some parallel universe. Every fellowship is ultimately local: part of a city, town, or municipality. In every spot that can be pinned on a map, there are birthing and dying, coming and going, working and playing, loving and hating, buying and selling, and sleeping and waking. Every locale has neighbours and newcomers, wealth and poverty, beauty and disaster, joy and lament.

Throughout this chapter we will use "city," but we do so for the sake of simplicity, recognizing that towns, hamlets, villages, and side roads are equally valuable God-given assignments.

Our city is the place we name when a stranger asks, "So where are you from?" Even in a large city, we'll name a place within the place when asked that question. If we're from New York City, we might name Harlem. If we're from London, we might name Camden. If we're from Nairobi, we might name Karen. If we're from Delhi, we might name Shahdara. If we're from Vancouver, we might name DTES (Downtown Eastside). Even the rural village I grew up in had its way of describing where people lived—even small-town streets and rural lanes are named.

What if the city is more than a place found on a map, or where we decided or were destined to do life? What if our city is an assignment given to us by Sovereign God?

In the New Testament, the Greek word for city is *polis* (a place of dwelling). It comes from the root word *polemos,* which means war or strife. Living in proximity can be a battle. *Polis* is also the source of the word "politics," which is not a bad word but at its best simply refers to the "affairs of the city." What might Sovereign God have in mind when he reconciles people like us to himself and brings us into the hope of his heavenly city?

Hebrews 13:14 says, "Here we do not have an enduring city, but we are looking for the city that is to come." The promise of eternity in Scripture is described as a city, a dwelling, a place where life happens and where God makes his dwelling with us. In the *polis* of God, we will be his people, his name will be our name, and his city will be our city (Revelation 3:12). In that city, God will wipe tears from our eyes and death; mourning and pain shall be no more (Revelation 21:1–4).

The Bible begins with a garden. The Bible ends with the promise of a city where God restores us to himself and his purposes and we live with him. In the garden of bliss in Genesis 3, a rupture took place that fractured everyone and everywhere. Every city feels what happened in the garden. From the city of God in Revelation flows a river of life with trees that will provide healing for the nations (Revelation 22:1–5). The new heaven and the new earth will include a new city that is a garden for the world. There we live *with* others and know *how* to live with others because the mayor is God himself.

Between the garden of Genesis 2 and the city of Revelation 22, the Bible dutifully names places people call home and live their assignments. Babel. Sodom and Gomorrah. Jericho. Hebron. Shiloh. Jerusalem (which means "foundation of shalom, peace, wholeness"). Nineveh. Babylon. Nazareth. Bethlehem. Capernaum. Ephesus. Philippi. Athens. Rome. The biblical accounts happen in places big and small, Jewish and Gentile, where languages, cultures, and ethnicities collide. Many of these places can still be visited and lived in. God's activity in history occurs where life happens, in places with names, identities, beauty, and the problematic impact of sin. This earthiness and authenticity are marvels of God's revelation of himself. He is the God who knows where people live, visits where people live, and sees the true reality of where people live.

Jesus saw what was really going on in Jerusalem. In Luke 13:1–5, Jesus used the city's headlines to highlight what people should pay attention to. The Lord referred to recent news of a sacrilegious execution of Galilean rebels by the Roman governor Pilate and the tragic death of eighteen caused when a tower fell on them. Jesus referred to these local sound bites to make a clear call: "Unless you repent, you too will all perish" (13:3, 5). Twice he stated it, as if to say, "The stuff in this city that you think is gossip-worthy headlines is calling you to pay attention to the direction of your own life! Are you paying attention to what the city is revealing about you?"

The city is the geography of home and comfort, homelessness and trauma. For many, it is a place of spiritual wandering. But it is where we live. Sometimes we learn from what happens in the bustle, and sometimes we are unaware of how the city is the corporate reflection of all of us. Sometimes we are oblivious to how unsteadily the city perches on the ledge of chaos and catastrophe. And at all times we are with a crowd of people we did not choose. But Jesus said he chose us and appointed us to go and bear lasting fruit, the fruit of the city of God that is to come, right here and now.

Should Christians simply ignore the city, doing our own thing and using the city for our own needs as we await that wonderful city that is to come? The biblical answer is a resounding "no!"

How we live in our city, in the neighbourhoods, parks, problems, and politics of the *polis* is a sovereign assignment. If God pays careful attention to so many cities, and even small backwaters like Nazareth that people thought nothing good could come from, then we must too. We who are made in God's image and have given to God what is God's are already citizens of heaven—our true passport—and the city that is to come—our true address (Philippians 3:20; Ephesians 1:18–23; 2:6, 19–22). But while we live with that identification and promise, we also live with the limits of our bodies and households in a terrestrial topography. We live here. And we are to live fully alive in that pinned point on the map where we spend most of our time as those who pray for God to light the earth just as he lights up heaven.

Let's talk about the politics of our *polis*. Consider these three arenas—national or federal politics, state or provincial politics, and city or municipal politics—through these questions:

Which of these receives most of your attention? Which receives the least?

Which of these receives most attention in the headlines that you read?

Can you name who represents where you live in each of those three political arenas?

If you are eligible to vote, have you voted in each type of election?

Where I live, in British Columbia, Canada, statistics reveal about 75 per cent of people participate in federal elections, 55 per cent vote in provincial elections, and between 30 and 35 per cent of eligible voters cast ballots in municipal or city elections. But where do we first live and have the most opportunity for influence? Is it not our city and municipality? To not engage in the city as a citizen is to look past it, to see it as existing for us, and to disregard our special responsibility for it. Those other political arenas do matter of course, but most people do not live in capital cities, and even Washington DC, Moscow, Berlin, Bogota, Ottawa, or Manila has a mayor and city-gate leadership.

The point we're making is not ultimately about voting itself, for we can be among the 35 per cent voting for our local city council member and leave our engagement at a pen stroke. The real question for ambassadors of Christ is this: Are we being God's ministers of reconciliation, fully alive citizens, and active contributors in the assignment of the city?

What can this city assignment look like?

In *Harvard Business Review*, Michael Jarrett describes four types of organizational politics.[10] His metaphors of the weeds, the rocks, the higher ground, and the woods can help us see how we can all influence our city.

- The weeds are the relationships and informal networks where we naturally grow up (as weeds do) to have personal influence. This is, for example, the parent group meeting in the parking lot to discuss a school issue or a group of co-workers talking over lunch about a work culture issue that could change or how their company could have a positive influence on the city. These relationships can have great positive influence, but, if we're not careful, they can also become negative and destructive.

- The rocks are the stabilizing power and influence we have, based on the title, role, expertise, or resources we have been entrusted with. This can be, for example, as a member of a community organization or committee, the coach of a youth sports team, the captain of that youth sports team, the foreman on a building worksite, or the nurse who can respond

---

[10] Michael Jarrett, *The 4 Types of Organizational Politics*, Harvard Business Review, n.d. (accessed May 19, 2023), https://hbr.org/2017/04/the-4-types-of-organization-al-politics.

to a medical emergency on the city bus. This is where we are expected to help and can strengthen the bureaucracies and institutions that are crucial for society to function well. Through these opportunities to influence, we help form the culture that makes city life better and more beautiful.

• The higher ground is the decision-making bodies where the policies and guide rails for everything else are determined and the rules are set. These are, for example, the elected student body council, local city council, the board of a not-for-profit organization, and other formal authority structures that are expected to understand the lay of the land, see the valley down below, consider various voices and factors, and guide the affairs of the city into goodness.

• The woods is the ability to discern, understand, and bring together the unspoken norms or hidden assumptions that are shaping the city so that we don't "miss the forest for the trees." For example, while many might assume that refugees live mostly in a specific area of the city, does it have to remain that way? Who will help bridge immigrants with the more established parts of the city to enrich everyone's life? Who will rally a neighbourhood to address the petty crime that is sadly being accepted as "normal"? Who will introduce strangers to one another, breaking down the fears that isolate people and cause them to misread and misjudge others?

Jarrett's metaphors are helpful and can help us see that "ambassadors of Christ" is not just a spiritual metaphor but a necessary role requiring tangible presences and practice. Regardless of our age, gender, or economic situation, we have opportunity to influence the city toward God's best.

Consider the Lord's surprising commissioning of the Jews captured and taken to Babylon in Jeremiah 29:4–7:

"This is what the LORD Almighty, the God of Israel, says to all those I carried into exile from Jerusalem to Babylon: 'Build houses and settle down; plant gardens and eat what they produce. Marry and have sons and daughters; find wives for your sons and give your daughters in marriage, so that they too may have sons and daughters. Increase in number there; do not decrease. Also, seek the peace and prosperity of the city to which I have carried you into exile. Pray to the LORD for it, because if it prospers, you too will prosper.'"

The Lord—who chose the Jews as the people through whom he would reveal his character and nature to the world and a Messiah for all peoples—had judged the Jews' unfaithfulness in their homeland. God mourned that Jerusalem had turned to other ways and gods. The once just and righteous city had become filled with thieves, self-seeking leaders, the chasing of bribes and comfort, and carelessness for the fatherless and widows (Isaiah 1:21–23). The city was, as all cities are, the reflection of the hearts of its inhabitants. The inner life of people always impacts the inter-life of people. After centuries of prophetic warnings, God allowed the Babylonians to destroy the city and drag the people of Jerusalem to a foreign city. They were not tourists but refugees and captives. How were they to live there?

When Russia's full-scale invasion of Ukraine began in February 2022, millions of Ukrainians fled their homeland. A pastor in Melitopol wrote a social media post to those in his church who escaped to western Europe. In a touching commissioning, he wrote:

While the first wave of Christian refugees to western Europe were met with flowers and red carpets and mayors, after a while that changed because not all those first emigrants behaved like Christians. You remember how we once welcomed refugees from Donetsk and Luhansk. You remember how disgusting some of them behaved. Then we understood their pain, anger, confusion, and shattered pride. You are now the refugees; behave in a new place in such a way that refugees from Melitopol are always and everywhere willingly welcomed! You will have a language barrier; therefore, it is your task to learn the language of the country in which you are! Learn the language from the first day! And a temptation will be to get everything for free! If you do this you will be overthrown. So, accept the kindness of others, but then earn money for yourselves following the example of the apostle Paul! You will also be tempted to envy; to want what the people of the new city have. But they have been creating their own well being for centuries! Initiative, hard work, and determination will help you. Manifest your best Christian qualities wherever you are! Bring the DNA of grace and the good of our city to all places. And may God help you in this![11]

He ended with a powerful postscript: "I did not post Bible quotes. This is your homework; finish it yourself." Do you think he might have been building them up based on Jeremiah 29?

Did you notice the details of the Lord's commissioning of the Jews in their new city?

- I sent you there—we are the first assignment (v. 4).

- Plant gardens—creation is part of the assignment (v. 5).

- Build houses and households—our household is an assignment (vs. 5, 6).

- Live and do as a fellowship—marrying and faith-building for the Jews was communal, fellowship life.

- Seek God's best (*shalom*, well-being, wholeness, peace, and prosperity) where I sent you—the city is our assignment (v.7).

---

[11] Accessed through a personal friend's social media repost in the weeks following Russia's full-scale invasion of Ukraine on February 24, 2022.

What does seeking God's best for the city look like? It looks like obedience to be God's representatives even when it is unwelcome and uncomfortable. It looks like doing the spiritual battle of tearing down strongholds through prayer. It looks like making this new place the best place it can be, unbroken and beautiful. The dominated Jewish captives were to bring the reflection of the heavenly city to the center of world domination. God's promise was that in seeking God's best for Babylon, the exiles from Jerusalem would find their welfare. Our own good is tied to seeking the good of the city of even our enemies. What an inspiring and challenging assignment!

Jesus commanded us to love the Lord your God with all you are and loving your neighbour as yourself (Matthew 22:37–39). When God's people, surrendered to his assignment of the city, seek the city's shalom, it is not only an act of love for God and neighbour, but of love for self. Our own welfare and good are bound to our neighbour's good. This is what that Ukrainian pastor was commanding his fellowship to be about as they were devastatingly forced from their hometown.

Consider carefully the order of the Lord's command to the Jewish captives:

- Accept this assignment as from Sovereign God, not from political upheaval or random circumstance.

- Establish creation-caring, faith-building, God-centered households that will multiply the aroma and difference of God's glory and presence through generations.

- Seek and contribute to what is best for the city you did not choose.

- Pray on the city's behalf, for many spiritual strongholds exist that no one else is praying against.

- When you live this way in the city, you will find the joyful *shalom* of God yourselves.

Are we are living like this in our city? Are we bringing this heavenly aroma into the weeds, the rocks, the higher ground, and the woods we have been sent to influence? Are we oblivious to Sovereign God's choosing and sending? Are we only seeking our own good and prosperity? Do we pray only for ourselves and never getting around to praying on behalf of this city God loves and knows? Are we demolishing strongholds of affluence, pride, loneliness, mistrust, depravity, violence, apathy, decadence, and selfishness? Are we seeking God's best for this place, even if we are despised?

The children of these captives became very influential. Yes, even the young can lead the way as ambassadors of the King of kings in the city. Daniel, Nehemiah, and Esther all lived this Jeremiah 29 vision in the affairs of Babylon and Persia in the years after Jeremiah sent his letter. The inhabitants of Jerusalem were commissioned by God to lay a foundation of peace and well-being in Babylon. They were the city of God in a city of idols. They were to heal and make it a city of peace (a "Jerusalem"). They were, in essence, to live the Revelation 22 vision that will one day be fulfilled in the city of our God!

Samuel Wells further helps us discern how to engage where we live as ambassadors of Christ in the city. In *Incarnational Ministry*, Wells says we can work for, be for, work with, and be with our city. But he cautions, these are not equally beautiful in the way of Jesus.[12]

Think of "working for," "being for," "working with," and "being with" like the temperatures a thermometer reads.

To "work for" is too hot! This happens when we see something must be done, and we dive in and do it *for* others. We may well-intentioned, even correct. Our action may even be grounded in love but ends up being presumptuous and rooted in the self-righteous belief that we know what's best for others. If we're honest, this is often about making us feel better and is too often selfish, overbearing, and controlling.

---

[12] Samuel Wells, *Incarnational Ministry: Being with the World* (Grand Rapids: Eerdmans, 2018), 12.

To "be for" is too cold! This is when we see something must be done and loudly broadcast that somebody should do something about it. The voice for change is often necessary, but clarity of the protestor can simply be cold and detached. It can push us to put a "thumbs up" or # on social media while never lifting a finger to help. It demands that government, the church, or an organization do something, but we remain critical bystanders, even if what we see is accurate.

Much warmer and effective for the city's good are "working with" and "being with."

In "working with" we labour shoulder to shoulder, mutually seeking shalom and well-being. We collaborate with common interest, working and praying through the challenges in the streets of *our* city. We seek God's best we seek as we work together with others, perhaps even those who do not believe as we do or even like us.

In "being with" we are together in the predicament and possibilities of our city. It's not a problem, or their problem, but *our* problem. It's not their neighbourhood mess, it's *our* neighbourhood mess. It's not their lament, it's *our* lament and we are with others in it. It is incarnational, remembering that Jesus promised his followers in his Great Commission, "I am with you always" (Matthew 28:20).

Jesus is reconciling all things to himself, including our city. What might happen if Christ's ambassadors and their fellowships would work with and be with their city? What if we involved ourselves rather than retreated? What if we did prayerful and spiritual battle to demolish strongholds? What if we were at the forefront of planning with others in neighbourhoods, workplaces, schools, and associations to bring God's best, his justice and righteousness, to reality even just a little bit more? What if all we could be was a night light in the darkness or a sprout of new life from the grey-brown dirt of winter? What if we celebrated where goodness arrived, reminding our city that whenever true beauty, justice, and right living are seen, they are signs of the reign of God that has come in Jesus Christ and will be fulfilled one day in the city where there will be no more tears or crying or death? What if we lived in such a way that we can be entrusted with more?

Back to Ukraine in the war of 2022. In the battered eastern city of Kharkiv those who couldn't or wouldn't leave were hiding in the metro stations, fearing for their lives and city. In that underground, sunless world, a city beneath the city teemed. Andriy, affiliated with the World Evangelical Alliance's Peace and Reconciliation network, wrote this after two weeks of endless barrage,

> "We are not going to leave. God has sent us here. The subway station … now has about 1,800 people. God gave the assignment to take care of the people who are there. I saw how much chaos and disorganization there was. I wrote down what and how we can organize and who should be responsible for what. I came with this proposal to the metro administration and police. They really liked the idea of bringing order and the head of the metro station appointed me to the role of internal manager. Pastors from other churches, after hearing about our successful ministry at the station, began to call and ask how they could serve in the same way. We are now serving in two more metro stations. These days I have met a lot of decent people with a big heart. I thank God. We will make a great feast with them after the war is over."[13]

Do you see how these ambassadors of Christ are receiving the assignment of their besieged city?

"We are not going to leave. God has sent us here"—we are being with!

"God gave the assignment … I saw … chaos. I saw what could be done. I saw the predicament and possibilities of shalom." "I came with a proposal"—I am working with!

---

[13] Accessed through a Peace and Reconciliation Network team member's email correspondence.

"Now other fellowships are joining in. We're now in two more metro stations"—we are partnering with others and living in such a way that we can be entrusted with more.

"We are planning to celebrate with a feast"—if not in this city, then in the city of our God where war will be no more.

Our city is the assignment; let us seek its welfare while we have breath.

## QUESTIONS FOR THIS ASSIGNMENT

- What do you love most about your city or town, and what are its biggest challenges?

- How does your household participate in the life of the city? Where do you love to go?

- Where do you have special relationships and opportunities in the city to serve as Christ's ambassador?

- How is the Spirit asking your fellowship to more intentionally participate in the life of the city?

# CHAPTER 8

# YOUR NATION IS YOUR ASSIGNMENT

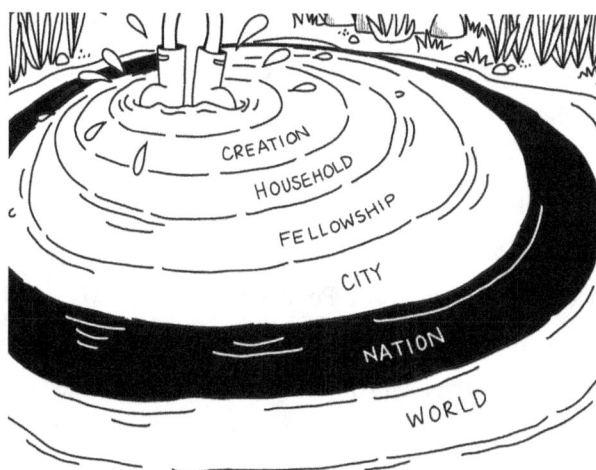

W e are, as Christ's ambassadors and ministers of reconciliation, the presentation of God himself with and within the unique limits and boundaries Sovereign God has given us. This includes many things we did not choose, like our family history, body type, birthplace, and intellectual or physical capacity. We can improve some things about us, but certain things are just the way they are. For instance, I'm never going to be six feet tall, Hispanic, or an economist, and I will have to deal with certain genetic dispositions and weaknesses. We all have certain constraints, but these do not stand in the way of God's desire to envelop us in his plan to fill the universe with his glory.

In John 9, Jesus sees a man born blind. The disciples wonder whose sin should be blamed for the blindness. "No one sinned," said Jesus, "but this happened so that the work of God could be displayed in his life" (see John 9:3). And then, rather disgustingly, he mixed his saliva with the dirt of Israel, put it on the man's eyes and healed him. Suddenly healed and a local celebrity, the man born blind was thrust into unexpected assignments. The rippling effects of the healing soon overflowed into his household, his faith fellowship, his city, and even the nation as the disruptive Sabbath-breaking scandal caught the attention of the Pharisees. The wonder of sight restored erupted into an attack on Jewish national identity. Until his personal encounter with the power of God, he was just a blind man, but suddenly his influence spilled over the banks of his simple, suffering life and into unexpected places. His life suddenly caused others to see the glory of God. Can all our lives have this kind of overflow?

I was about fourteen when I attended my cousin's wedding in the United States. On Sunday morning, the day after the wedding, we worshipped with a church in a Pennsylvania town. My buddies and I hung out with that fellowship's youth. The awkward adolescent tension was finally broken when an American girl made a pointed observation and accusation: "You guys have hockey accents!" What did that mean? I didn't even realize I had an accent! Furthermore, what on earth was a "hockey" accent? Was there a land called "Hockey" that I was unaware of? (If so, at that point in my life I would have emigrated forthwith!) As Pennsylvanians, our new friends' primary exposure to Canadians was the professional hockey players they heard interviewed on television, and since many professional hockey players are Canadian, we sounded like those guys. To an American ear, I had an accent, but not even a Canadian one—a *hockey* one. I was a stereotype! For the first time, I felt that I was not only from someplace else, but I was someone else.

What does it mean to be of a nation? Is it always what is assumed or stereotyped?

My friend Lennett is pastor of a fellowship in Nova Scotia on Canada's Atlantic coast. I live on my country's Pacific coast. We are of the same nation state but could not be much further apart. He leads a congregation that began as a community of freed Black slaves who were refugees in 1794, before there was even a country called Canada. My white European ancestors didn't come to Canada until around 1850. So if I assume that to be of my nation with a Maple Leaf Flag is to be white with a "hockey" accent, I'm naively presumptuous. In fact,

Japanese, Chinese, and Punjabi people settled in the region of Canada where I now live long before I arrived. And of course, Indigenous peoples called this land home for thousands of years, stewarding the hills and waters before Jesus saw the man born blind on the streets of Jerusalem.

All around the world, we find ourselves limited by borders drawn arbitrarily, occasionally hastily, and often by the victors of a conflict, well before we were born and granted citizenship. But our country, part of the United Nations, is now ours to steward with those who have resided a long time or a short time. As Christians we must accept that in this moment Sovereign God has given us an assignment in this nation, no matter how it came into being, how we got there, or whether we like it or not.

In Scripture, nations are peoples, not borders as we memorize them on colourful political maps. They are not necessarily nation states as we think of them, but peoples created and loved by Sovereign God. Three New Testament Greek words give us understanding.

The first, *ethne* (root of "ethnicity"), means people with similar customs, culture, and language (like Ukrainians or Jamaicans or the Rohingya).

The second, *demos* (root of "democracy"), means people bound together by similar laws and organized politics (like my country, Canada, which is made up of different ethnicities, or like South Sudan, one of the world's newest states). The ancient Roman or Babylonian empire fits this category: a form of organized politics that was an umbrella over many peoples (*ethne*). Over time, such a politically organized *demos* can become a broadly shared and influential culture. The New Testament was written in Greek because Greek culture had flooded the Mediterranean world even as far as India by the time of Jesus because of the empire-building of Alexander the Great generations before Jesus was born. While Greek was the widely accepted written language of the region, Jesus spoke Aramaic, a language that emerged as Hebrew, Edomite, Phoenician, and other Semitic languages mixed over centuries. Similarly, today English has emerged as a dominant tongue that much of the world uses in some form, but that has not always been so, nor may it always be so.

The third New Testament word, *laos* (root of "laity") means an unorganized people at large. It is a people who share a place or geography in general.

Consider all this for our own country. In general, we are a *laos* (a people) trying to figure out life together on the same geography. We are bound together as a *demos* (a political state) by a connection to the organized structures that have been shaped over time. And we are many *ethne* (ethnicities or people groups) who have accents, skin colours, traditions, customs, and ways of life not everyone else shares. Together this is what a biblical view of the nation is like: people in relatively the same place, organized by a shared political structure, and made up of different and unique ethnic groups.

God is ultimately interested in people. While he ordains or sovereignly puts in place political structures and rulers (*demos*) for periods of time to bring order, the Lord wonderfully celebrates and does not obliterate what is different about the ethnicities made in his image. Jesus said to his disciples, "Go and make disciples of all nations, baptizing them in the name of the Father and of the Son and of the Holy Spirit, and teaching them to obey everything I have commanded you" (Matthew 28:19–20). The "nations" are the *ethne*, the unique peoples that need to be brought home to the Father who loves them as they are and seeks to reconcile them to himself so they too can be his ambassadors. Jesus commanded that his way of life be embodied within all the ethnicities of the world to express the glory of God through each culture, bringing their unique God-given strengths to their moment in history. Our Christian assignment is to pay attention and help our unique people group (*ethne*) contribute to the political state *(demos)* to make life more like heaven for all the people *(laos)* who dwell here.

Sovereign God rules and ordains nations for his purposes; even when it doesn't make sense to us. We might think God can only use certain rulers we approve of, but in Isaiah 45:1 God even calls the emperor Cyrus of Persia his "anointed" (Hebrew word "Messiah"). Yahweh had a purpose for Cyrus that was bigger than an emperor's political ambitions. In the New Testament, Christians under persecution are reminded that there is no authority except that which God has established (Romans 13:1). God uses political powers to order the chaos the world can spin into. He will also use those powers in ways we think impossible and improbable. After all, it would be by the order of Persian emperors that the Jews returned to rebuild Jerusalem, and under the *pax Romana* (the peace of Rome) and its incredible network of roads that Christianity had unexpected opportunity to spread.

In Genesis 11 humanity faced a towering challenge despite what appeared to be a startling collaborative engineering achievement. In the long shadow of the tower of Babel, God confused human speech, preventing human culture from becoming disastrously and selfishly monotone and monochrome. At Babel, humanity sought to rise to divinity and make a selfish name for itself. Humanity pined for unity, but not with one voice for the glory of one God. We were determined to raise our own voice, not seek the whisper of the creator. God in his grace scuttled this vanity. God's diversifying of people, wrote Dietrich Bonhoeffer, "is a divine institution which causes mankind to live in dissension and mutual incomprehension, and which thereby reminds men that their unity does not lie in their own achievements of complete power but solely in God, the Creator and Redeemer."[14]

We were created and blessed to steward what was God's, living joyfully by God's family name and purpose since we belong to the creator. God's initiating of a systemic and political fracturing in

---

[14] Dietrich Bonhoeffer, *Ethics* (London: Collins, 1963), 345.

Genesis 11 saved the world from the human propensity to believe our own headlines and rule and unite wrongly. The gift of diversity rescued us from the costly slavery of uniformity that destroys human dignity and robs God of the glory he seeks to reveal through the wideness of his creation in partnership with his goodness. It was on the cross that Jesus destroyed that which divides the nations (Ephesians 2:14). Our common creator united us himself and unites those in every nation who humbly seek him. And when the Holy Spirit came upon Jesus's disciples at Pentecost, human speech was reunited for heaven's purposes while maintaining beautiful cultural uniqueness (Acts 2).

After Babel, God invited Abraham and Sarah to leave their country, kin, and household for a land they would be shown (Genesis 12:1–3). God promised that through their descendants all the families, peoples, and nations of the world would be blessed. From this defining moment those who know God are to be a blessing to the nations, no matter what land or epoch they find themselves in.

This—not the technicolour coat—is the real story of Joseph at the end of Genesis. As a descendant of the God of Abraham, Isaac, and Jacob, his father, Joseph brought blessing to Pharoah and Egypt. Egypt could spread a table of salvation in a time of widespread starvation because Joseph responded to Sovereign God's plan for him in Egypt, even when it didn't make sense. Egypt was eventually eclipsed as a world power. None of the great empires in Scripture lasted. Kingdoms rise, fade, and some fall hard. History follows this pattern. As Daniel 2:20–22 says,

> "Praise be to the name of God for ever and ever; wisdom and power are his.
>
> He changes times and seasons; he deposes kings and raises up others.
>
> He gives wisdom to the wise and knowledge to the discerning.

He reveals deep and hidden things; he knows what lies in darkness, and light dwells with him."

Light—the way of life—dwells with God and all nations, and even great empires need life and light.

Hundreds of years after Joseph and Daniel, the apostle Paul debated in the influential city of Athens. There he said the nations have a common origin, rooted in God's plan, with set boundaries, limits, and allotted periods, in order that they will seek God and find their way home to him (Acts 17:26–27). Despite all the polling, noise of news channels, and bluster of social media, we can forget that kingdoms rise and fall. God is in control. Sometimes the rising of a nation brings about God's holy purposes in this sinful world. Sometimes the falling of an empire does it. We must, therefore, have a first allegiance to the great King of all. We must keep our eyes on Sovereign God, as Joseph, Daniel, Esther, and the early church did, so that we can continue Abraham's blessing in our nation assignment.

God wants the nations to see well. God's people are to be a window through which they can see God and his ways. When God organized the descendants of Abraham—the Hebrews—into a nation, it was not to fly their own flag, but so that among all the nations of the world, there was a people flying God's flag.

The Israelites were an enslaved people without power formed by the choice of Sovereign God and his grace in delivering them from Egypt. They were a miracle. The law was given to shape Israel into a people who showed the world what the living God was like. They were to have no king. The unseen God was to be their supreme ruler. Living God's commands would show what the great King was like. They were to be the nation through whom God would reveal himself for all peoples as Messiah (Isaiah 42). The law also exposed Israel's inability to do this by their own strength or ethnic superiority. The law exposed the nation's sinfulness and stubbornness and that the only way to be part of God's purposes was by humility, repentance, deliverance, and the Spirit of God. Over and over, God saved his people from their blundering mistakes and blatant evils. Meanwhile, the sacrificial system reminded them over and over that redemption and reconciliation was never cheap.

Isaiah 2:3–5 trumpets that God's people were to be a different kingdom other peoples could turn to when nationhood was a mess:

> "Many peoples will come and say,
>
> 'Come, let us go up to the mountain of the LORD, to the temple of the God of Jacob.
>
> He will teach us his ways, so that we may walk in his paths.'
>
> The law will go out from Zion, the word of the LORD from Jerusalem.
>
> He will judge between the nations and will settle disputes for many peoples.
>
> They will beat their swords into plowshares and their spears into pruning hooks.
>
> Nation will not take up sword against nation, nor will they train for war anymore.
>
> Come, descendants of Jacob, let us walk in the light of the LORD."

God's people stick close to God as they live among the nations and are sometimes swallowed up by them. They become like God, are aware they are not God, are not building a kingdom of their own, yet always point like faithful ambassadors to God's good and transformative reign. In the Bible, God's people serve various national political powers as his ambassadors so that God's best can be realized everywhere—as Jeremiah described to the exiles in Babylon.

Abraham lived this out among neighbouring kings greater than he. Joseph and Moses both served Egypt, albeit in different ways. Joshua figured out life among many nations. The judges and kings struggled to live as a window of God's best with Philistines, Assyrians, and Babylonians. Daniel was a cabinet minister in Babylon where he practiced his faith in Yahweh at great cost. Esther was in a forced marriage with the king of the world's greatest pagan empire.

The entire New Testament was delivered under the umbrella of the rule of the Roman Empire, a Caesar-worshipping, Greek gods–invoking monstrosity of a political system that demanded loyalty and crucified traitors. And all through this grand adventure, God's people—those shaped by God's different way—are to focus on the shalom of God's kingdom while they engage the various political realities of their own day. In the New Testament, there is no attempt to impose a particular "Christian" political system, but there is always a desire to serve and open a window to the shalom and reconciliation of the God so that the nations born blind can finally see.

In the assignment of our nation, Christians always live with a great tension: We obey God rather than human authority (Acts 5:29), *and* we accept being subject to governing authorities (Romans 13:1). The apostle Peter told Christians enduring suffering to submit to governments which are placed by God and focus on doing good for the sake of the greater nation (1 Peter 2:13–17). This was living truly free and a sign and witness of God's reign. Such faithfulness silences the accusations of evil and ensures that God's salt and light peppers society. Paul instructed Christ's ambassadors to pray for kings and all in high positions, that peace may prevail, God's kingdom may be witnessed to, and everyone may come to the knowledge of the ways of God (1 Timothy 2:1–4).

We hold the tension tight in the assignment of our nation. We obey God ultimately if a political power sets itself up as god and against God, commanding us to stop proclaiming and demonstrating the gospel of the King of the nations. And at the same time, we honour the authorities Sovereign God has chosen. We seek the good of all, pray for government, and conduct ourselves as the best citizens because we are first and foremost citizens of heaven. Having given to God what is God's (ourselves) we can give to Caesar what is Caesar's. We are ambassadors focused on God's shalom and good news. We serve our state, resist the temptation to be the state, while prophetically reminding the state that Caesar is not God.

Jesus lived this before Pilate (John 19:1–16). When the governor bluntly reminded Jesus of his power to release or crucify him, Jesus bluntly reminded Pilate his authority only came from above. In fact, Jesus was submitting to that higher power on the way to crucifixion, which would bring freedom from sin for Jews and Gentiles, whose authorities both wanted him dead. Jesus demolished the strongholds both Jews and Gentiles had erected and served. The political debate with Pilate was a mere pit stop on the journey to form people from every nation who could serve God's shalom within every nation.

Though some expected it, Jesus did not ignite a political revolution against Rome. He created something more revolutionary: a new humanity from every *ethne*, *demos*, and *laos*, which would reveal the shalom of God with the beautiful uniqueness of each one. Jesus lived, died, and rose within the limits of a political reality so that God's good news could be revealed for all people through people like us.

Jesus brought God's reconciliation into the diversity of his own nation. Jesus responded to a Roman centurion's faith, even though he represented the newcomer and oppressor Jews didn't like or want (Matthew 8:5–13). He strategically sent the twelve disciples to the lost sheep of Israel, where they were to focus on those who were like them (Matthew 10). Further along in Matthew 15 he served a Canaanite woman, the neighbour who was not like them but was among them for a long-time (and even on the land before they got there). Jesus served each of these within his own nation. He was demolishing strongholds, building up people, responding to faith wherever it was seen, even in people the Jews thought they had nothing to learn from (like a centurion, a Canaanite woman, and the hated Samaritans).

Jesus saw people and peoples. After all, how the nations live really, really matters. How nations live affects people made in God's image and the societies they create. Titus was given an assignment on the island of Crete, an island nation with a long history and peculiar ways. Paul was clear with Titus that discipling this ethnicity wasn't easy, for Cretans described themselves in very plainly: "One of Crete's own prophets has said it: 'Cretans are always liars, evil brutes, lazy gluttons.' This saying is true. Therefore rebuke them sharply, so that they will be sound in the faith" (Titus 1:12–13). Paul is quoting the philosopher Epimenides of Crete who lived around the sixth century BCE. For generations, Cretans had built a proud reputation and culture that would not be easily undone. But the ministry of reconciliation was desperately needed because how Cretans live really, really matters. The Cretans were aware of behaviours that were far from best yet were strongholds that were accepted as "just the way we are."

What is written about our people or nation?

What do our own philosophers say?

What about us needs transformation?

After all, how our nation lives really, really matters.

In Matthew 25, Jesus points to coming judgement with a parable about the separation of sheep and goats. The sheep fed the hungry, visited prisoners, and clothed the naked because it was the just and shalom thing to do. They didn't even realize they were doing this for Jesus and to Jesus. They were rewarded with walking into the pastures of eternal life. The goats were those who didn't do such acts of shalom goodness. They were selfish and blind, and they went away into eternal punishment.

Who is being judged in the parable? It is not individuals, but nations. "When the Son of Man comes in his glory, and all the angels with him, he will sit on his glorious throne. All the nations (*ethne*) will be gathered before him, and he will separate [them] one from another as a shepherd separates the sheep from the goats" (Matthew 25:31–32).

Judgement will come on the nation that is our assignment. How our nation lives really, really matters!

How will the nations become sheep? God's strategy to transform nations is God's people. Those who embody the ways of the King who came and will come again are to disciple the peoples into their God-given purpose for the good of God's world. This is our ambassadorial task: to help goats become sheep and form a more just nation. This is a miracle only God's Spirit can accomplish. In a sense, every nation must be delivered from Egypt. Our assignment, therefore, is not a particular brand or system of politics. Our assignment is to witness to, speak for, and embody God's kingdom so that goats become sheep. We are to be healing to the nations.

This requires demolishing strongholds through the spiritual warfare of prayer and gently but courageously unraveling the arguments set up against the knowledge of God. Strongholds such as the Cretans had accepted. Strongholds that must be seen in the light of the gospel and the way of Jesus the Messiah. Strongholds of nationalism, ethnocentrism, xenophobia, racism, love of power, individualism, pride, and rebellion need to come crashing down. Our ambassadorial task is not against people but against the spiritual forces of evil in the heavenly realms that seek to suppress the beauty of nations and use them for their sadistic ends (Ephesians 6:11–12).

We must also build people up. We must be with and for our nation so that God's goodness shines. We need to be not less but more connected to other Christians of different ethnicities and denominations in our country. We must pray for and encourage our nation's leaders toward a more just and whole society. We need friendships of mutual understanding in the pluralism of our globalized contemporary societies—including befriending people of other faiths and secularists who claim to be the "nones" (no faith tradition). We need to be known as encouragers, truth-tellers, lovers of the poor, peacemakers, and lavishly generous people. We are not ashamed of the gospel of Jesus but neither shame nor despise those who do not believe as we do. We must be rightly engaged in the political system of our nation—not stoking revolution so that the nation is made in our image but seeking a recovery of sight and healing of the peoples. Christians should be the ones offering solutions to the problems and predicaments the nation is facing and seeking answers for, not those creating the problems.

Finally, we must live so we can be entrusted with more. Our task, writes Miroslav Volf in *A Public Faith*, is "to help people grow out of their petty hopes so as to live meaningful lives, and to help them resolve their grand conflicts and live in communion with others."[15] This means we who now see and are led by the Holy Spirit must stop our pettiness and purposelessness and live as reconcilers in all our assignments. We must maintain our saltiness and keep the lights on. Our good deeds should glorify our Father in heaven, who has many children among many nations. We should live in such a way that we will be asked to do more, even if ridiculed and persecuted for righteousness's sake (Matthew 5:10–12). Even if, as in other times, Christians are hated because of Jesus (John 15:18), we must live in a such a way that when the nation convulses or crumbles, faith, hope, and love remain. We must live in such a way that in the wildest national chaos there is a proven community that can be trusted to seek the good of all and who are skilled at forging ploughshares from swords.

Our ambassadorial assignment in our nation is to be that beautiful people who are more joyful, lamenting, faithful, loving, shalom-building, and prayerful than anyone else and can be asked, "Take us up to the mountain of the Lord. Teach us his ways. We want to walk in his paths."

---

[15] Miroslav Volf, *A Public Faith: How Followers of Christ Should Serve the Common Good* (Grand Rapids: Brazos, 2011), 100.

## Questions For This Assignment

- Where do you or your fellowship have opportunity to actively serve your nation?

- What national issues do you most care about and pray about?

- What people groups within your nation do you have special care for or relationship with?

- How is the Spirit asking you to live in the tension between obeying God and honouring government authority within current national realities?

# CHAPTER 9

# YOUR WORLD IS YOUR ASSIGNMENT

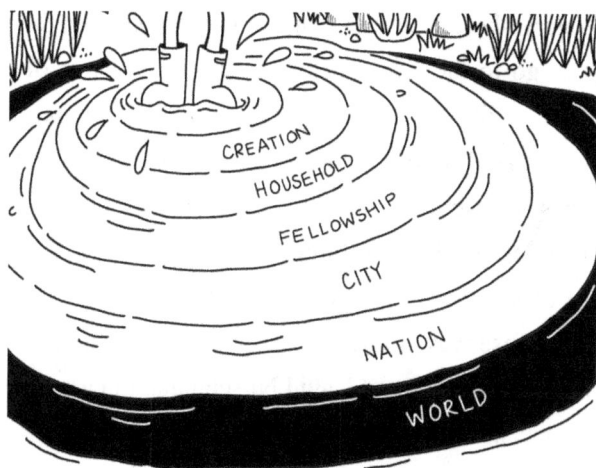

After splashing through other assignments, we finally arrive at what may seem way too big: the world!

I feel like I can barely manage the assignment of me and my household sometimes. How can I possibly have responsibility for the world!? Do you feel that way? Remember, however, we have been learning a geography of life that is unique to the limits and boundaries of our created gifts and personalities, where God placed us, who he placed us with, and our historical moment. After all, 1922 was not your assignment, and neither was 1722.

Speaking of 1722 …

In 1722, Count Nicholas von Zinzendorf welcomed persecuted peoples from Moravia and Bohemia (eastern Czechia and Slovakia) to his estate in Herrnhut (today's eastern Germany). Religiously those who came were Lutherans, Calvinists, Roman Catholics, Free Church, and Anabaptist believers who were looking for a peaceful place in conflicted times. By 1727, a rich communal life shaped by Scripture and prayer emerged. Round-the-clock prayer began in 1727 that, believe it or not, lasted a hundred years! All this produced incredible fruit as this unlikely fellowship of a few thousand people began an unprecedented response to the needs of the world.

Known as the Moravian Brethren—or *Unitas Fratrum*—they dispersed everywhere. It was not uncommon, of course, for European Christians to go to the world in those days, but it was often tied to expansion of political empires. The colonizing church produced blurred lines, mixed motives, and practices with fateful and lingering consequences. The simple Moravians were very different.

When an escaped West Indies slave arrived at Herrnhut, the community awakened to the horrendous treatment of Africans. The Moravian response was almost unbelievable: two ordinary guys, John Leonard Dober (a potter) and David Nitschmann (a carpenter) made a stupendous decision. On October 8, 1732, the two boarded a ship for the West Indies. They would sell themselves into slavery to be with and work with the oppressed. Compelled by the love and ways of Jesus, they chose to suffer at the hands of their fellow Europeans for the sake of those very different. Within eighteen months, Dober was dead. Nitschmann pressed on. Soon, other Moravians joined him. By 1737, an intercultural church was born with Caribbean slaves baptized into the same fellowship as Europeans for the first time.

Soon, Moravians could be found scattered throughout the Caribbean, Greenland, South America, India, Africa, the United States, and Canada. They did not see countries or empires; they saw nations (*ethne*) and went to them throughout the world. They often suffered along with the Indigenous peoples they befriended. The Moravians were an unlikely marvel: a community of Christians pushed into the world by a divine hand. They faithfully took their assignment of the world seriously and received their marching orders from the Lamb who had overcome.

"For God so loved the world that he gave his one and only Son, that whoever believes in him shall not perish but have eternal life. For God did not send his Son into the world to condemn the world, but to save the world through him." (John 3:16–17)

God loves the world. Not just the world to come without war or pain, but the world as it is with its good, bad, and ugly; its laments, sorrows, and sin. God loves the world because the streams, valleys, and cattle on a thousand hills are his. Because we are here.

God sent to the world. God came to the world. Not just to save people out of the world, but to save and engage the world that is. This is the same world his ambassadors and ministers of reconciliation have responsibility for. As the Father sent the Son, so we are sent into the world. We are to take the world seriously as he does. When Jesus prayed for us, he asked, "My prayer is not that you take them out of the world but that you protect them from the evil one. They are not of the world, even as I am not of it. Sanctify them by the truth; your word is truth. As you sent me into the world, I have sent them into the world" (John 17:15–18).

The New Testament Greek word for "world" is *kosmos*, which describes the ordered system of this planet that thus far keeps spinning. It's the word from which English derives "cosmos"—normally thought of as the expanse of galaxies where the Hubble telescope peers. It's also the root word for "cosmetics," the ordering, assembling, or putting together of the face of things. This world has much that needs more than cosmetic work—more than the false, airbrushed reality we humans tend to give it. The affairs of this world need to be adorned again and again in the image of the creator.

God's love for the world is good news for all that is on this planet. That God loves me, my neighbour, and my enemy is glorious, hopeful news. That God is concerned for great cities like Nineveh and small country hamlets like Punkey Doodles Corner and seeks to fill the universe with his glory, calling us to humbly live faithfully within the limits of the assignments he has given us, is quite staggering, is it not? After all, have you listened lately to the news of the world? The Holy

Spirit awakens ministers of reconciliation to the reality of those who may not be like us, may be far away, and may be far from God or closer to God than we are. If the world is God's loving assignment—and the scope of his sending mission—then the world beyond us is somehow our assignment too.

Returning to 2 Corinthians, we hear this stirring in the apostle Paul,

> "Neither do we go beyond our limits by boasting of work done by others. Our hope is that, as your faith continues to grow, our sphere of activity among you will greatly expand, so that we can preach the gospel in the regions beyond you. For we do not want to boast about work already done in someone else's territory." (2 Corinthians 10:15–16)

Paul, a Jew, deeply longed for the maturing work of God in his mostly Gentile hearers to overflow to regions beyond Corinth in southern Greece. Greece was already a long way from where Paul grew up. It was also a long way from where the Christian movement had begun only a few decades earlier. Already by this point the church was moving toward the "ends of the earth." Paul even told the Christians in Rome—where he had never been—that he hoped to visit them on his way to Spain (Romans 15:24). This wasn't to bask in the Mediterranean sun, but to follow Jesus into a global assignment. This desire for the world by a very small group of people with little political power (not unlike Moravians in the eighteenth century or Tajiks or Ugandans in the twenty-first century) should not really surprise us.

Why do Christians go to the world?

First, because of identity and identification. Logically, if God loves the world, then those who respond to his love and follow Jesus would find their identity as children of God too and identify themselves with their Father's love for the world too. This is woven through Scripture. The world and its people belong to God (Psalm 24:1). The Jews were chosen from the ends of the earth to be God's people (Isaiah 41:8–9).

That chosen-ness was lavish, undeserved love (Jeremiah 31:3). Yet the Jews were not chosen because they were more special than others (Deuteronomy 7:7). They were chosen for the sake of the nations (Isaiah 42:5–7).

From the ends of the earth God calls the unlikely and undeserving. We're all far from him at some point. To the ends of the earth God sends his children that the world may be filled with the knowledge of the Lord as the waters cover the sea (Habakkuk 2:14). God loves. God's love compels him to pursue, even if his wooing is rejected (Hosea 3:1). God's love received and growing in reconciled people will compel those who are now his family forward into the world as well (2 Corinthians 5:14).

A harmonic song of heaven erupts as a response to wonder at the Lamb who was slain and alone is worthy to rule the world,

"You are worthy to take the scroll and to open its seals,

because you were slain, and with your blood you purchased for God persons from every tribe and language and people and nation.

You have made them to be a kingdom and priests to serve our God, and *they will reign on the earth.*" (Revelation 5:9–10, italics added)

Saints from every tribe and language, every *laos* and *ethne,* receive the assignment from the Lamb to be priests and ambassadors. They identify with the One who reigns forever, and they reign on the temporal earth as the presentation of God himself. This is the unlikely identity Christians have in the world.

Second, Christians go to the world because of the breath of God. Jesus promised, "You will receive power when the Holy Spirit comes on you; and you will be my witnesses in Jerusalem, and in all Judea and Samaria, and to the ends of the earth" (Acts 1:8). The Holy Spirit, the indwelling presence and power of God, literally blows Christian proclamation and demonstration into the cities and towns we inhabit and to the ends of the earth.

Ah, the ends of the earth: that's where explorers want to go!

In March 2022, Sir Ernest Shackleton's ship, *The Endurance,* was found at the bottom of Antarctica's Weddell Sea. Shackleton's ill-fated 1915 British expedition to be the first to cross Antarctica began with dreams of glory and ended up with his ship locked in ice and eventually 9,842 feet underwater and his men adrift for months. It's an amazing tale of human survival.

What is it about human beings that makes some want to go to the ends of the earth? Why do high school grads want to backpack to places unknown? Why are some people longing to take a vacation to the endless expanse of space? Why would Brazilians desire to plant churches on cold North American prairies? Might this thirst for exploration be rooted in the image of God? Might it be that we have a responsibility for more than just where we are? Might it be that something has been planted in us for the "ends of the earth"? The Holy Spirit that dwells in us will blow unlikely people and their Spirit-led fellowships into unexpected world-spanning adventures! In fact, if we are not blown into the world in some way, we should probably ask if we are paying attention to the Spirit of God at all.

I was once in the Panamanian jungle at the end of the Pan-American Highway. There, Wounan and Embera Indigenous tribes (who once destroyed each other) form a family of churches, operating a discipleship school for their youth. That school is led by a Colombian couple—Einer and Girlesa—who left their homeland to serve tribes that do not trust Hispanic people because of the trauma of colonial history. This Colombian couple so loves these tribes that they have adopted a boy who was born from Wounan and Embera parents. In fact, they were asked by the communities to raise the child as a sign that they belong to both peoples now! When I visited, a young man and his wife wanted to talk because they knew I was from Canada. They had experienced a long partnership with a Canadian church built on friendship and mutual blessing and shared their deep desire to serve Indigenous people in Canada with the same love of Christ they had received and understood.

From where do Colombians discover the assignment to Wounan and Embera tribes? From where does a young Indigenous couple receive a vision to love First Nations peoples in Canada? This assignment of the world is rooted in God and our identity in him, which comes alive when we are led and formed by the Holy Spirit in all our assignments in such a way that we can be entrusted with more.

Not everyone will be like Paul the apostle or Thomas the disciple, who eventually ended up in India. Very few of us will be like Einer and Girlesa or that young Wounan couple. But that does not mean the world—the places beyond that God longs to fill with his glory—is not our assignment. Some of us may very well be given an assignment in the world from God through our vocational calling in business, medicine, education, agriculture, or a trade. We may awaken to our assignment in the world through travel, where the "real" Dominican Republic or Indonesia discloses how shallow our life is and messes with the comfortable world we have assumed. It may be that our fellowship sees more in us and sends us to go on assignment somewhere else.

The love of God is uniquely communicated and demonstrated when someone, as if blown by an irresistible wind, crosses cultures and border for the sake of another place and people—like Dober and Nitschmann, like Einer and Girlesa. It's one thing to love our own nation; it's quite another to love those who are not like us, to embrace them, to be with and work with them, to bless and nourish the flourishing life for a nation not one's own.

Jesus's words echo through the centuries to his disciples throughout the world,

"I tell you, love your enemies and pray for those who persecute you, that you may be children of your Father in heaven. He causes his sun to rise on the evil and the good, and sends rain on the righteous and the unrighteous. If you love those who love you, what reward will you get? Are not even the tax collectors doing that? And if you greet only your own people, what are you doing more than others? Do not even pagans do that? Be perfect, therefore, as your heavenly Father is perfect." (Matthew 5:44–48)

This is the nature of the complete and perfect love of God: a love for the stranger, the "other," even the enemy. This is the love that begs the question, "Why?" Why do such a thing? Why would a community somewhere else in the world love us? The answer for ministers of reconciliation is this: because of the compelling, Spirit-blowing love of God!

Have you ever considered that apart from someone from somewhere else taking seriously the assignment of the world, you would never have known Jesus Christ? God disrupts the dysfunctional lostness of the world as people who surrender to the blowing of the Spirit embrace regions beyond. That's why, even if we never leave the city or rural route we were born in, we have an ambassador's assignment in the world. Considering carefully, we will make the surprising discovery that God has put the world in our hearts for his glory.

Don't think so? Perhaps a few questions might help:

- Is there news from a particular place beyond your own country you track with interest?

- Is there a person or friend somewhere in the world you have kept in touch with, even though you rarely if ever see them?

- Is there a place beyond your own country you are increasingly curious about, even if you've never been there?

- Is there a place beyond your own country you have visited or always wanted to explore, even if you can't explain why?

• Are there movies, documentaries, or books from a part of the world you are drawn to?

Notice any patterns? Are any "ends of the earth" close to your heart?

Now what are our tasks in this assignment of the world?

First, **we demolish strongholds**. We pray for that place. We pray consistently for the spiritual strongholds that are binding a place to be brought under the reconciling lordship of Jesus Christ. A clue to the strongholds can often be found in reading history and headlines. Strongholds can also be exposed, believe it or not, in the way we stereotype the people of the world. Stereotypes are often belittling caricatures, but they do exist for a reason.

Consider this joke about Europeans, which contains unfair generalizations as well as just enough irreverence to shake loose a chuckle: "Heaven is where the cooks are French, the police are British, the mechanics are German, the lovers are Italian, and everything is organized by the Swiss. Hell, on the other hand, is where the cooks are British, the police are German, the mechanics are French, the lovers are Swiss, and everything is organized by the Italians."

Have we ever wondered how others stereotype us and why? What do the comedian's provoking jokes about us reveal? Perhaps what's being noticed about our part of the world would expose strongholds in need of demolition too.

Remember how Paul reminded Titus that the Cretans were liars, evil beasts, and lazy gluttons (Titus 1:12)? Would those patterns be overcome merely through reading *Five Steps to Avoid Lying, Tame the Evil Beast, and Get Off the Couch?* (Don't search for it; the book doesn't exist.) Spiritual work and warfare are non-negotiable in the face of strongholds and destructive patterns in the parts of the world God has seeded in our hearts. You don't need to be in Ukraine, Russia, South Africa, Panama, or the United States to demolish strongholds there. If a part of the world has your heart, don't just read the news, pray the news!

Second, **we build up people**. If you know people in another corner of the world, do you talk to them? Have you learned from them so they can build you up? Have you encouraged them with a text or a call? When Russia invaded Ukraine in 2022, I watched my wife give hours connecting with and building up friends in Ukraine who were in crisis. She couldn't go there, but she could still take her assignment seriously in that part of the world. In a globe shrinking thanks to technology, everyone everywhere can build up people somewhere.

You can also build up people by welcoming and supporting those who go where you can't. The New Testament implores Christians to welcome those who are servants of Jesus from other places and send them on their way with blessing.

> "Dear friend, you are faithful in what you are doing for the brothers and sisters, even though they are strangers to you. They have told the church about your love. Please send them on their way in a manner that honors God. It was for the sake of the Name that they went out, receiving no help from the pagans. We ought therefore to show hospitality to such people so that we may work together for the truth." (3 John 5–8)

Does your home welcome the world? Are your finances blessing the world? Is your money helping to build up people somewhere else? Beyond humanitarian and compassionate aid, we can stand with people who uniquely represent us and have been blown by the Spirit into regions beyond for the sake of Jesus. Investing financially and relationally in Christ's ambassadors who go where the limits of our lives keep us from going is one way to embrace our assignment of the world.

And perhaps you should seriously give prayer and communal discernment as to whether God is sending you or someone from your fellowship to build people up somewhere else. Not as a tourist or to chase an experience (though God can grab your heart that way). Not to escape home (because everywhere you go, there *you* are). Not to fix the world (because you're not that smart). Not for your sake, but to be with and work with. To build up people because the Spirit has blown, and the love of Christ compels. This going across cultures is one of the costliest things anyone can do. Still, ambassadors of Christ should ask: Is there a stirring in me for a region beyond like Paul had for Spain, Einer and Girlesa had for Panama, or that Wounan couple had for Canada? Might my skills and expertise be needed elsewhere? Might I be a bridge for that people group to bring God's shalom blessing to my part of the world? And at the very least, what do I need to learn to cross the intercultural boundaries of the world that exist right where I live?

Third, **we live in such a way that we can be entrusted with more**. Paul humbly acknowledged that how he lived among the Corinthians, and the heavenly fruit being produced in their lives because of his assignment with them, was what gave him authority to go to regions beyond. The longing to influence regions beyond is directly related to the integrity of our lives in the community that has experienced us. Some desire to change the world but have no faithful track record, patient endurance, resilient maturity, or humble teachability in their other assignments. They have not demolished strongholds or built up people where they are. As a result, they are not to be trusted in regions beyond. How we live in God's other assignments is the gateway to ends of earth.

So we come full circle: back to the assignment of you! Have you—whether young or old, female or male—given God you? Sovereign God seeks kingdom ambassadors and ministers of reconciliation in every sphere of life. He is calling you from the ends of the earth, for the sake of the ends of the earth, that his glory may fill the universe.

Consider yourself summoned.

Live your assignment.

## Questions For This Assignment

- What places and peoples of the world have your attention?

- What global issues do you most care about and pray about?

- How might your household or fellowship discern and embrace a global assignment?

- How is the Spirit awakening you to something or somewhere in the world that you have not considered to be an assignment before?

# A Commissioning
# into the King's Parade

One of the small towns our household called home had an annual Christmas parade. Our house, with its long front porch, was situated on the main parade route. Every first weekend of December we sat there in the chilly pre-winter darkness as local business and community organizations' floats crawled by with glittering lights. Because it was a small town, bystanders knew almost everyone who waved their mittens as they went past. These Christmas parades build to the crescendo of Santa Claus, who always rides in last. As he "ho-ho-ho"s and shouts, "Merry Christmas!", children's eyes widen. Meanwhile, the adults squint, trying to discern who is behind the synthetic beard and wearing the red suit this year. Everyone knows that when Santa Claus rolls by, the parade is over.

One year, however, in a blustery snowstorm that some thought would cancel the parade, the unexpected happened. As Santa slid by, the eyes of all turned to what trundled behind him. There, plowing determinately through the snow-thickened street, was an eighty-year-old man we all knew riding a three-wheel battery-powered scooter. He was stoic and calm, his gaze straight ahead. He was as if sent on assignment. He completely stole Santa's jolly thunder. No one could quite tell if this was part of the plan. What was he doing? Who sent him there? Whose idea was this? Is this what we all waited for? Was there more to come? It was awkward and wonderful all at the same time. And this grandpa's peculiar presence created the Christmas parade our household would most remember and talks about still.

"Thanks be to God, who always leads us as captives in Christ's triumphal procession and uses us to spread the aroma of the knowledge of him everywhere." (2 Corinthians 2:14)

Like today's parades granted to a city's championship team, or like military parades that roll through the world's capital cities to demonstrate might and dominance, ancient Roman generals were granted a triumphal procession. The focus of the parade was the conquering hero. Riding high on his valiant chariot, he would be honoured as *vir triumphalis* ("man of triumph") for the rest of his life. Coming behind the triumphant warrior would be evidence of his victories—the captives and spoils of war that were proof he had overcome.

Paul turned this ancient parade of domination on its head. Christ is the victor! The Lamb of God has overcome. He is reconciling all things, demolishing the strongholds, and building a new humanity, and the expanse of his kingdom and reign will not end. It is *his* parade. And Paul was proud and thankful that those who had surrendered were captives bringing up the rear to catch the eyes of all. Jesus, crucified by Rome, is the man of triumph, and we who are the ordinary, the humble, and the unlikely with limits and limitations are spreading the aroma of his victory everywhere. We ride in his wake. We are voluntary recruits. We are compelled into the parade by love. We are the fragrance of the King. The crowds who look upon him now look to us to see what he has accomplished.

Because of Christ, God has adopted orphans and proudly named them his daughters and sons. He has transformed sinners into saints. He has created a new humanity from the warring divisions of Cain and Abel and Jew and Gentile. He has by the miracle of grace genetically reengineered goats into sheep. He has converted enemies into friends. He has made heaven's opponents into ambassadors of his reign.

We are captives commissioned into Jesus's victorious parade. We spread his aroma in the assignments he gives—ourselves, creation, our household, our fellowship, our city, our nation, and our world. We may seem odd to those who gawk, but like the octogenarian stealing Santa's spotlight, when we show up and live our God-given assignments, people will know the parade is not over, and there are vital tasks yet to be done by everyone everywhere so that the glory of this King fills the universe.

So go boldly and fragrantly into your assignments, O you ambassadors of reconciliation; you are commissioned into your King's parade!

**PRN** Peace & Reconciliation Network

A commission of the World Evangelical Alliance (WEA)

The Peace and Reconciliation Network is a Commission of the World Evangelical Alliance and exists to inspire and equip the church and people of peace to enable communities to live life in all its fullness.

PRN asks, "What if every local church was a center of reconciliation?" and then works with regional and national Evangelical alliances around the world to see the work of peacemaking and the ministry of reconciliation become a central component of the mission of the church everywhere.

PRN seeks to strengthen the four dimensions of reconciliation centered in Jesus Christ as found in Scripture: reconciliation between God and humanity, reconciliation with ourselves, reconciliation with others, and reconciliation with God's created world.

To learn more or have a PRN leader, like Phil Wagler, serve your community go to www.reconciledworld.net.

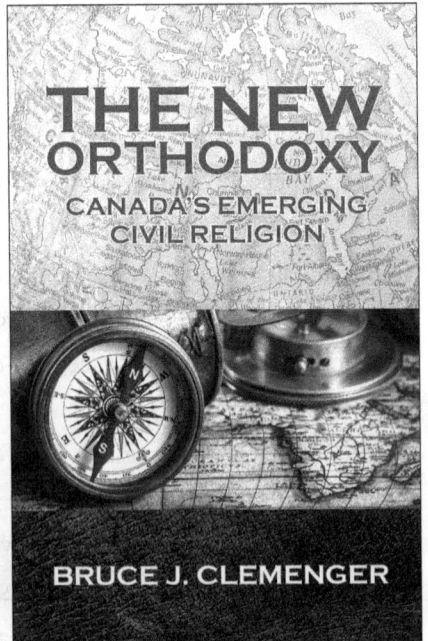